the Cow Whisperer

by
Skip Halmes

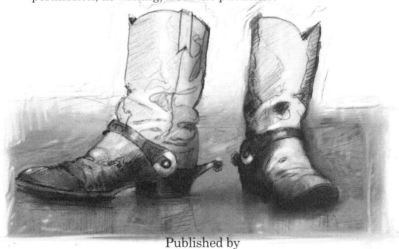

Published by
Quixote Press
1854 345th Ave
Wever, Iowa 5265

*This book is dedicated
to my family.*

PREFACE

My family and I live in a very rural part of west central Montana. Many of the small towns out here have a weekly newspaper and ours is the *Cascade Courier.*

These papers keep us informed of local news, important events, and school sports. Our paper, like most, has area writers that write a weekly column on their specific area's news and happenings.

Our Mission Road region didn't have a writer so a few years ago I took on the position. The first week or two the neighbors were happy enough to talk to me, but then, they soon tired of it and I was mostly an annoyance. The biggest problem by far, however, is that almost nothing happens to write about. You just can't make the yearly ranching routines sound very exciting.

On one of my weekly news gathering phone calls I asked one of my neighbors, "What's the news?"

"There ain't no news; and if I did have any I sure wouldn't tell you. You'd put it in the paper."

So I just started telling stories on paper and this is the best of them. They were very popular. I love to make people laugh and these stories were all done to spread a little cheer: I just hope you have half as much fun reading this as I did writing it.

There is a key to a true treasure of wisdom in these pages, and **when you seek** this out, **you will find** some extra laughs and insight. So many people told me to write a book that I was finally convinced, and I sure hope you enjoy *the Cow Whisperer.*

Table of Contents

CHAPTER ONE

Mr. Mom

*L*ast week I took our pre-school son, Matthew, to story hour at the library and visited with some of the ladies over coffee and cookies. This is nice but not nearly as fun as the good old days when I would meet other captains of industry at the Driftwood Bar and enjoy refreshing beverages while discussing the complexities of the cow business, politics, or elk hunting.

Our life has taken on a lot of changes since I sold my brokerage business in Great Falls last May, and I've been home almost every day. Last fall my wife, Holly, decided she had better get a part-time job, being concerned that our small cow herd and new outfitting business was going to starve us to death. She is so pessimistic. Our kids were doing just fine on chokecherries and elk meat, and we sure didn't need to go to the gym.

I have discovered numerous helpful recipes and timesaving ideas in my short time as Mr. Mom, and I think the reason Holly seems so dour and surly lately is that she didn't think of some of these ideas herself. Take, for instance, my method of feeding our three- year-old Matthew and one-year-old Katie breakfast. I simply scatter Cheerios across the kitchen floor as you might feed the chickens. The food will wind up there anyway, and I accomplish several functions simultaneously. This provides a meal, keeps them busy, and really aids in their hand eye coordination. A small side benefit is that it has certainly given little Katie an understanding of the rigors of competition. You ought to see her when they hand out cookies to all the children at the daycare center - she's quite the little scrapper.

Another gem is my recipe for tater tot surprise. I simply take all the leftovers from the week before and dump 'em in a cake pan, mash 'em down good, and sprinkle tater tots across the top. Bake it at 350 degrees for 20 minutes and salt to taste. Depending on what you've had the week before, you usually get the three major food groups, and it might make its own creamy sauce. I never could figure out what Holly did all day. I would come home from a grueling day of business lunches, phone calls, or task delegation, and it looked like she was exhausted. After all, she only managed three small children, fed the cows, and cleaned an old farmhouse. I will concede we ate a lot better, and all wore clean clothes, but other than that, it's been no big adjustment.

Her adversarial attitude towards my household duties and the scope of my new responsibilities has worried me to the point that I may appear a bit frazzled myself lately and has started to under-mine my once rock-solid confidence. Where I see my methods as thrifty and efficient, she thinks I'm cheap and lazy. She just turned 30 last week so it must be those female hormones I read about in my new subscription to *Women's Day* magazine that has so darkly altered her personality.

Just yesterday she arrived home from her cushy job as a recovery room nurse, and her timing was awful. The kids were fighting over a piece of toast they found under the stove, and I was trying to stay current on a particularly intriguing episode of my favorite TV series--- "Baywatch".

Immediately she starts with the angry interroga-tion. "What do you constantly find so fascinating about that stupid show?"

"Duhh – There's some damn good life saving tips and water safety info on there."

"Ya -- like the buoyancy properties of silicon. Have the kids had anything to eat today?"

"Don't get your tail in a knot," I said. "We finished off that bag of Kitt Kat bars left over from Halloween. The ones with the nutritious cookie center."

She squinted meanly and persisted in her interrogation. "Did you send Jacob to school in his footy pajamas again?"

"Hey, he had his pants and boots on over the bottom, and besides, I couldn't find any socks!"

"These kids are filthy. Did you ever even once consider using the washing machine?"

"Sure, but every time I turn it on they keep jumping out the top."

Then there was great wailing and gnashing of teeth, - sorta like when we eat tater tot surprise.

Proverbs 17:1

CHAPTER TWO

Bad Gas

*L*ast week my wife, Holly, (a neatness freak) was cleaning out the freezer. Her process involved grabbing clumps of frozen stuff, holding it out for my identification, and then throwing them away.

"What's this thing?" she scowled.

"It's a frozen calf hide. I thought I might be able to graft a calf on to that good young cow whose calf I ran over. I saved the dead calf's hide, but it was starting to stink, so I froze it."

"That cow dried up a month ago," she snapped.

"Well, I thought it might make a neat throw rug, " I offered.

WHACK WHACK THUMP WHACK THUMP.

When I tell the boys down at the bar that Holly missed me, it usually means that I was able to duck a left hook. Unfortunately I'd rolled the hide up to freeze it, and she used it like a club to beat me about the head and shoulders.

She was attempting to pound some sense into me, and it must have been working because I started thinking. Trying to cover up a mistake or laziness with quick thinking has not proven very fruitful for me in the past, and, in fact, has led to a lot of unnecessary pain and suffering. I either need to work on my delivery, to seem more believable, or improve my skills in self-defense.

One such unpleasant occasion that comes to mind occurred the second year we were out on this ranch. The brush had really taken over, and I was cutting it, piling it, and setting the piles on fire. It was on a Saturday, and my mom had driven out to visit. She is a widow, and I have always felt protective of her since my dad died. A gentleman had accompanied her, and I didn't like him. He dutifully walked down to my present brush pile to say hello, and I gruffly acknowledged him, trying to convey he better not try any funny stuff with my mom. In fact, I felt pretty damn tough that day. Here I was with my shirt off, sweat glistening off my rippling love handles, and armed with my big Jonserude chain saw. As I loomed under him, I thought I was a formidable presence and was probably very intimidating. In my own objective opinion, this present gentleman friend of my mom's wasn't much to brag about. When he looked at you, one eye was fishing and the other was diggin' worms. He was of questionable lineage, donned a Bozo-the-clown haircut, and wore an ever-present comical expression. He smelled like a lounge and I knew I didn't want to spend the next umpteen holidays passing him the turkey.

It was a hot day, and I had a jug of water. I also had a jug of chain saw gas.

As you might guess, I was so busy looking tough that I didn't look. I just reached down and grabbed the jug and tipped it up. When the gas hit my mouth, I realized in horror my mistake. A normal person would have spit it out, asked for medical assistance, and sworn off smoking. Not me, I did my best to convey that I drank chain saw gas quite regularly. I noted the wild look of astonishment in his eyes, tipped the jug back down, and passed it to him, as if he might want a little taste himself. To his credit he declined. He then assumed a defensive posture and stepped back a couple feet.

"You must really be thirsty. That --- that stuff is no good for you at all," he said.

I casually shrugged my shoulders and stood there with that gas in my mouth looking as tough as I could, without spitting, for what seemed an eternity, while he droned on about the weather, baseball teams, and his first-hand knowledge of the perils of unnatural chemicals. The sixties had been real good to this guy.

He finally sensed that I was not in much of a mood for conversation and sauntered off to the house. By the time he left there wasn't much gas left in my mouth to spit out. I had a terrible heart burn, my watering eyes crossed, and my body had achieved an octane level far superior to the effects of three-alarm chili. The phrase "bad gas pains" had taken on a whole new meaning.

The silver lining in this little incident is that it led to one of those special moments my mom and I shared. I had never admitted my little *faux pas* to Mom or anyone else, and I hoped she would come to her senses and ditch this guy before he ratted on me. She voiced her concern over how hard I'd been working, all the stress of my job, and, mostly, the affinity for petroleum products that she'd been told I had developed.

She opened the awkward subject quite delicately by saying, "My boyfriend, Floyd, told me he caught you drinking chain-saw gas."

"Aw, Mom, don't worry, that's just an old cowboy trick I use sometimes. I can't believe he fell for it. You let 'em watch you have a little nip of a toxic substance, and then they avoid your whole gene pool. Saves the problem of havin' 'em for relatives later on."

She then winced sharply and wrinkled her nose under her cat-eyed glasses, as if she were scrutinizing the evidence, and said, "You know that's a lot like what your cousin, Mel, said when they caught him drinking sheep dip. Then his hair turned orange, he got his ears pierced, and he converted to Republicanism."

She had located a facility in Wyoming that had agreed to accept me. They have a proven eleven-step program where they start you out on super unleaded and wean you down to strong grain alcohol in only eight weeks.

CHAPTER THREE

Preg Testing in His Sleep

We are all sure enjoying the nice weather - just right for calving season. My whole family is very excited with the news of my nephew being accepted to Convenience Store Management school.

My sister went to check out the learning facility over in North Dakota and she said, "It's really the Ivy League of lower learning and they have a special rate for team ropers. He's going to minor in fast food frying techniques. The school has very strict standards, and they must have an I.Q. that's higher than their age." She then told me about some of the courses - Mixing Slurpies 102, Resetting the Gas Pump 203, and collecting video fines. For this class they have some Sicilian fellow named Big Lou to offer some helpful tips that have proven fruitful for him in his own collections career.

I wish sometimes I wrote the news for the other side of the river. All kinds of newsy things happened over there this week. A good friend of mine from over on Adel Road has a big gash on his mouth and a couple busted teeth. He says he had "an accident in the shop," but I've had enough frying pan treatments myself to recognize one when I see it. I'm not surprised at all that this happened to this particular guy. He has the very annoying habit of doing his next day's work in his sleep the night before. I've been in cow camps with him where he'd be snoring, gathering cattle, and ordering men and dogs around all night long, so you can imagine how disquieting it must be to try to sleep next to him.

Well, they were supposed to pregnancy test some of their cattle the next day, so use your own judgement as to what happened. He has suffered some terrible wrath, developed a nervous twitch, and says he is still not sleeping too soundly.

This guy's wife is a no B.S. kind of gal who recently won a pie-eating contest at our county fair. I think, the next time his cattle have to be treated for sunburned bags, he better sleep downstairs for awhile.

As for the husband-of-the-month, it's our local veterinarian, Dr. Cowvorkian, hands down. My sources tell me he was seen pulling his new bride, seated in their canoe, across the ice in their yard. The treacherous condition was caused by the recent ice jam from the Missouri River, and he pulled her between their front step and the safety of their luxury car. What a vision, can't you just see the stalwart vet pulling his adoring wife while she urged him on with spirited words of encouragement, and a stock whip. I get all choked up just thinking about it and it sure sets a tough standard for the rest of us.

I wish I could say that events were as splendid in my own marriage. Between this employment forced role reversal we have undertaken and the little mishap my wife suffered with the hormone implant gun when we were branding our calves, something is really straining our partnership. I don't mean to sound less than perfectly objective, but it's all her fault. At least she doesn't have any ugly mood swings anymore. She just stays mean and surly all the time. She cares nothing for my needs or of quality one-on-one time for conversation. She seems more interested in football games and the performance of her Harley. Also next year she wants to kill her own elk. Besides her being more aggressive and insensitive, I think she has started to put on weight.

When I subtly brought these issues to her attention she vehemently disagreed, stuck her fist through the wall and said, "I'm only retaining fluids."

From our tab at the Driftwood Bar I strongly suspect it's in the form of draft beer.

Proverbs 21:9

ANDYMAN

insulate basement

can buy direct
cturer or visit
om on the Web.

to buy a pellet
ur home. We
are brands. We
erested in the
, the motor and
e looked online
port of any kind
hings and found
tell us where to

to all that trou-
e availability of
ea. Also under-
have a pellet
out of heat any
goes down. If
a good local
u also will find
ood, practical
. Remember,
equipment is
closest, reli-
r. If it's win-
equipment
need reliable
you cannot
do not have

a viable heating choice.

Q. *We had a huge pine tree
against our house in the back yard.
Two windows are on either side.
The tree was cut down, but I can't
get the windows clean. The resin or
sap or whatever seems to be em-
bedded in the glass, and when the
sun shines on the windows, they
look terrible.*

A. Go to the Gordon Food Service nearest you and get a can of
their spray foam window cleaner.
It is the same product as Gleem,
which you can get at some, but not
all, janitorial product distributors.
The product is a combination of
three different alcohols. Use a 100-
percent cotton cloth when window
cleaning. Paper toweling and am-
monia-based window cleaners just
streak. If you are not near a Gordon's, you can get Gleem on the
Web at *www.dudco.com.*

*Send questions to: Ask Glenn,
Master Handyman Press, P.O. Box
1498, Royal Oak, Mich. 48068-1498
or send an e-mail: askglenn@mas-
terhandyman.com.*

Gannett News Service

ving

H

CHAPTER FOUR

Love and Money

A lot of you would think I might have made some people a lot of dough with shrewd stock picking techniques or precision market timing in the futures and stock market back when I was a broker. In fact, I did help a few people out, but this is a story that took place long before that. This is how I kept my best friend from becoming a millionaire due to my bad advice.

We lived down on the outskirts of Bozeman in my rundown mobile home complete with aluminum siding, bad shag carpet and a self-styled addition. I broke horses, worked at the fairgrounds, did some horse trading, and whatever else I could for money while I was going to college. I was poor. I had no feminine attention or prospects for any. My best friend and roommate, Dudley, was a handsome cowboy. His family had a big ranch. He always had more money than me, and he acted and looked like Clint Eastwood. He was a top hand with horses, and he had a silent Scotch demeanor. The more scotch he drank, the meaner he got.

Dudley's girlfriend lived right down the road. She was a beautiful, only child of a wealthy man. To facilitate her interest in horses, while she attended college, her dad bought a horse farm. He built her an indoor arena and renovated the house and out buildings.

"Now there is a guy who knows how to take care of his kid," I used to tell my dad.

The other sickening thing about this story was that if Dudley wouldn't have had this girlfriend, there were plenty of others he could have lined up.

This was a stark contrast to my own romantic situation. I had acquired my only girlfriend through illicit means. She was a T. A. (teaching assistant) who instructed a chemistry lab I was taking at college. I was trying to charm my way into a better grade in the lab, and one thing led to another. I was always going to trade up, but she got around to it first and left me for some nerdy guy that looked like Kosmo Kramer.

Bridgett was a tall, blond Polish girl and a throw-back to an old-time hippie. We called them "earth rangers" in those days, as it was more politically correct. She rode her bike everywhere. So to help win her favor I got a bike and some glacier glasses and started pedaling to school. This saved me a lot of gas money, but it sure scuffed up my cowboy boots. She didn't shave her legs either. The first time she wore cut-offs I thought she had on angora chaps. We had a philosophy class together starting at seven in the morning, so I'd start off on my bike extra early, riding the nine miles to campus so I could buy us two polystyrene cups of "Morning Thunder" hippie tea, that she was fond of. The stuff tasted like you soaked an old leather glove in a cup of hot water, and it gave me gas. The people who concocted that tea probably had a sense of humor and that's how they came up with the name.

As you can see, my romantic situation was grim and held no promise. I have no idea what possessed Dudley to ask me for advice on the subject. He did, though, so the outcome is partly his fault.

Here's where I get to the meat of the story. It was during finals week, and Dudley had been extra sullen. I had been breaking a mare down at his girl-friend's place and noticed that this snappy-looking horse trainer from Canada was staying down there. I surmised that this was the reason for my partner's discontent. He wanted to go to the bar to talk. While we are there drinking whiskey, he explains that this handsome horse trainer with the fancy rig and horses is her old boyfriend, and Dudley is concerned about how platonic the whole situation is.

I love to be asked for my advice and to appear sage and wise. The trouble is that I'm not that smart and rarely have anything intelligent to say. This, however, has never stopped me from dispensing a portion of my rambling thought process whenever possible.

So I say, "It seems to me what's killing you is not knowing. If a guy knows they are together, and you're history, you could deal with it. Or if they're not, you could handle that, too. It's this not knowing that will eat you up."

Dudley nods in agreement. He's hanging on my every word, and so, poised with confidence, I go on.

"It's one in the morning. Let's stop in and see who is sleeping where, and that will give us our answer."

Dudley agrees it's a hell of an idea. After a couple more drinks, away we go. We are parked in the driveway, and before we go charging in the house, he wants me to slap his face.

"Why?" I asked.

"Because if I am going to fight, I want to be good and mad!" Dudley shouted.

"No!" I protested.

"Do it!" he shouted again.

WHACK. I hit him.

"Do it again," he said.

WHACK....WHACK...WHACK.....WHACK.... WHACK (He had coyote-like out-maneuvered me on a previous girlfriend deal so I got in a couple extra licks while I could.)

"OK. Enough already."

So now, sufficiently stimulated with the appropriate degree of discretion we are primed for our slightly less than objective meeting with Dudley's girlfriend and the Canadian horse trainer.

We barge in the door like a couple D.E.A. cops on a high-profile drug bust. The Canadian horse trainer jumps up off the couch where he has been innocently sleeping. Understandably, he thinks we are up to no good and goes to step in front of Dudley. So Dudley knocks him down. This shouting and scuffle attracts the attention of Dudley's girlfriend, who comes downstairs wanting to know what the commotion is all about. Dudley tries to verbalize his emotions and explain but doesn't do very well. She looks to me for answers. I start thinking. If I could just appropriately express Dudley's passion and concern for her affections, I could salvage the relationship. He could still get hooked up with this millionaire's daughter and reap the benefits of a huge shortcut in life's journey. Or someone - maybe even someone like me - might.

"Hey, I tried to stop him," I shrugged.

CHAPTER FIVE

The Tough Shit Ranch

I was taking care of our three-year-old daughter, Katie, last week, and she was watching the Walt Disney classic, "Bambi". I noticed the theme seemed to be herbivores were thoughtful gentle creatures, while the carnivores, including man, were evil, snarling, fiendish brutes. The movie shows all the happy Forest animals living in harmonious bliss and portrays the biggest buck as a wise caring leader who's known as the Prince of the Forest. I remember when I first saw "Bambi" when I was young. I thought the Prince of the Forest was a nice buck, too. A buck with good mass, a nice wide spread, a little weak in the tines, but certainly something I'd like to lay low with my old thunder stick.

Before you judge me too harshly, let me explain a chapter from my formative years. When my sister and I were growing up on the ranch, my dad and grandma would "buy us" some calves every winter from a dairy. Dairy calves were very cheap in those days and we would either mix them up powdered milk replacer or force a dairy nurse cow to stand for several strange calves to suck on her.

This process involved chasing the cow into a corner of the corral, brandishing a big stick, and a lot of loud threatening curses when she'd kick at one of the calves. It's how a lot of ranch kids learn to cuss. Now, you might have assumed since these calves were purchased for us, we would share in some of the profit from this operation - not so. We got hollered at when one died or got sick, but they were only ours to take care of.

As you might imagine we became quite fond of some of the calves and we always named them. Snuffy sniffed a lot, Buttons had special markings, Beauty was pretty, and so on. These calves would follow us around. Some became pets, but it never ended well.

Every year, usually late in the summer, early one morning it was time to butcher. We'd have to help with that, too. Breakfast, afterwards, was always a pretty somber affair.

"Pass the eggs, you murderer," I'd snap at Dad.

"Dad shot Frisky," we'd sob to Mom.

My dad, like most parents then, was always attuned to our happiness and immediately sensed we were upset and needed to address the issue of our conflicting emotions. NOT.

"What the hell's the matter? Ya think we should just eat the ones that die of old age? Frisky was a good steer, and Porkey was a good pig, right down to the last bite. Now quit whining and pass the bacon."

So it came to pass that we understood at a very young age that meat came from animals, and sympathy came from your Mom. It's not that my dad was unconcerned; he was a great father. It's just that he was very busy and there was a lot of work to be done that took precedence over our emotional bruises. With today's standards, if I would have had a sharp lawyer and a rich dad, I could have probably sued him for a traumatized childhood or pet mutilation, but I was busy too. Parents in those days thought that if you were loved, fed, clothed, and warm, they were meeting all of your needs, and the answer to most issues was to work you so hard you forgot about your other problems.

"Dad, I don't think I'll make the cut for the basketball team."

"Gee, that's too bad. You better go load the truck with hay bales to build those muscles."

"You're getting a D in chemistry! Go chop the ice out of the water holes, you should have plenty of time to figure out the reaction between water and freezing cold air while you're doing it." And so on.

When I was about 17 I was trying to break a colt named Jug. He bucked me off at least once a day and I hated him. Dad thought that if I rode him enough he'd get over it, but it was taking that S.O.B. a long time to get tired of bucking me off. One day he bucked me off on a barbed wire fence and it cut my left hand quite badly, and Dad had to

take me to town to get it stitched up. The next morning I was supposed to move some cows on the same horse and, when I was just swinging on, he took off bucking. Well, I couldn't ride him on a good day, and that day trying to hold on with my newly injured hand, I didn't even warm him up. Dad saw the horse running around without me on him and came over to the corral.

I was so mad and frustrated with that sorry horse that I just sat there pouting, right where that horse had bucked me off. Now, you might think my dad would offer some encouraging words like, "I thought you'd ride him that time," or "That new contusion above your left eye sure complements your olive complexion."

Instead - and this really happened - he said, "You're sure not doing that colt any good by letting him buck you off all the time."

So you can see that it's sorta bred into me not to be too sympathetic, and I guess I'm not. My wife, Holly, calls our place the "Tough Shit Ranch." Ya get skinned up, "Tough Sh-t," some of the calves die, "Tough Sh-t," and the list goes on.

The first choice of treatment for nearly any injury on our place is a stern lecture on safety. My wife is a recovery room nurse, so it's pretty hard to impress her with the severity of your present wound, but that doesn't keep us from trying. She has seen the consequences of carelessness and takes it very seriously. When one of us gets injured around there, an initial consideration is: Will the first aid be more beneficial than the butt chewing will be painful?

I've told her when she was correcting our kids because of their dangerous antics, "Don't hurt 'em worse than they were gonna hurt themselves."

I don't know if cowboys' hats squeeze out the last remaining sympathy genes or if their demented idea of humor masks the feeling, but what a sick group we are. We'll be watching some poor guy riding his bucking horse through the brush and laughing our heads off.

"Ha, hee, hee, I sure hope he doesn't get skewered by one of those big sharp sticks that are poking up all around him when he falls off."

"Boy, Steve, that was really funny toward the end when you hollered so loud while that horse was standing on your ear."

Take, for example the action-packed videos titled "Rodeo Bloopers." They should be called "Nightmares for Cowboys."

"Bloopers"- as if the cowboys and the bulls playing tetherball with the contestant's heads are just out for some lighthearted fun. I love the narrative.

"What a hoot, looks like he'll need at least one prosthesis and reconstructive surgery after that thrashing. Look at that. Ol' Slim is taking a little nap in the arena. Hardee-har-har- hee." It's sick.

As a former bloopie, I can assure you it's no fun at all, and some of those guys are scared to death. They say there are not any atheists in foxholes, and there aren't many behind the bucking chutes either. If you get badly injured or knocked unconscious, your friends drag you out of the arena and ask you questions to try to determine the extent of your present brain impairment.

"Do you remember you still owe me gas money?"

Or to determine if you require hospitalization. "Do you have insurance?"

Team ropers have a great sense of humor, too. When one of them lose a finger or thumb to the rope, their partners jeer, "Old Leroy is gonna have to use both hands to order five beers from now on. Hee, hee-haw."

Matthew, our five-year-old, loves to ride a bike. Last summer I backed my pickup over his bike where he had left it lying. We had told him repeatedly to put it in the shop when he was done with it, and we didn't think we'd teach him anything about responsibility by immediately replacing it. (You know it is the Tough Sh - t Ranch.)   In order to get to ride a bike he has to use his older brother's, which is too big for him.

His system for riding this oversized bike is to hold it up along a salt block, to start out, and then peddle like mad. His theory is there's no substitute for momentum, and, of course, he wants us to watch him ride. Inevitably he has to get off, and because his legs don't nearly reach the ground, it is always a tip-over crash landing. With his mother and me screaming to be more careful and go more slowly, he always gets up no matter how badly he's skinned up and states, "That didn't hurt."

He's at a very reckless stage, and since he gets in trouble for injuring himself or not being more cautious, about every fifth sentence of his is "That didn't hurt."

This fall when we took our horses and mules up to the hunting camp, Matthew was riding our oldest mule, Molly, in the round corral in front of the barn. I had poured some pellets in the feed boxes for some horses we were going to shoe. When Molly heard this, she decided to come in the barn at a trot. WHACK. Matthew's head hit the beam over the sliding barn door. His hat brim had hidden the beam from his view so he hit it pretty hard, but it didn't quite knock him off the mule.

When his head popped back up, his big brown eyes were really watering and he said, "Now **THAT** hurt."

He's gonna fit right in on the Tough Sh-t Ranch.

CHAPTER SIX

Dear Skip

*B*ecause last week's column spoke so much about horses and the cowboy lifestyle, several readers have written with questions. I'll answer them the best that space and my ability will allow.

Dear Skip,

My horse is a 14-year-old mare named Princess. She is half Arab, 1/4 Appaloosa, and 1/3 Shetland. The problem is this - every time I try to mount her, she jumps by me and kicks me in the stomach. I'm real nice to her and give her sugar cubes or apples and pet her whenever she lets me. Sometimes she bites me or tries to strike me, and it really hurts my feelings. What should I do?

Signed,

Wounded in Wolf Creek

Dear Wounded,

Obviously you have been insensitive to Princess's needs and should have been more kind. She is now rebelling. My suggestion is to sell her to a local horse trader and hopefully he will find her a better home. Don't be too concerned if he wants to weigh her before he pays you. It's the cowboy way.

Dear Skip,

Why do you buckaroo types still wear those pointy-toed boots with the big under-slung heel?

Signed,

Baffled in Bozeman

Dear Baffled,

As with most cowboy styles and gear, there is really a practical application. Being very foresighted people, the bootmakers have noticed that cowboys are evolving into truck drivers. The under-slung heel is designed to be the ergonomically correct angle to easily slide on the floorboard to run the gas pedal. If we miss a few payments on our truck, the bank has these repo guys confiscate it and its contents and lock it in an impound lot. The lots are guarded and enclosed by a high, diamond-patterned, chain-link fence. These fences are very difficult to climb with round-toed footwear.

Dear Skip,

What are your thoughts on corrective shoeing?

Signed,

Ima Farrier

Dear Ima,

I have mixed feelings on the subject. Just yesterday my three-year-old son came to me complaining his feet hurt. When I examined him, I was thrilled to see that he was suffering from a mysterious condition causing his toes to point out, just like all the great bull-riders do. When I looked more closely, I noticed sadly that his feet were normal, and he only had his cowboy boots on the wrong feet. I wanted to leave them the way they were, to aid in his toes-turned-out development, but changed my mind to appease my nit-picky wife.

Dear Skip,

What is a Horse Whisperer, and what do they do? Also I've been reading a horse-training book and there are a lot of technical terms. What is a leg Que?

Signed,

Confused in Cascade

Dear Confused,

Horse whispering is a very useful skill in the equitation world. Last week I thought I should put some miles on one of our dude horses because she had become so fat and cantankerous. When I started out she bucked and threw a fit. First, I whacked her down where the colt sucks, and then I whispered in her ear.

"The meat works is paying fifty-eight cents a pound for horse meat."

Worked like a charm. It may be helpful for you to hear these terms in context. I'll help you with a fill-in- the-blank quiz.

Suppose you saddle up a colt for the first time, and as you cinch him up, his knees buckle. If you kick him in the guts, that's a leg _____.

If you are in the local bar misbehaving, and your wife hits you in the head with a stick that is hanging on the wall, that's a pool _____.

If the colt you're breaking turns out like the mare in the first question, hopefully a canner buyer will send her to packing plant and the Frenchmen can have a Bar - B _____.

CHAPTER SEVEN

The Hail Mary Cow Release Method

*I*t has sure been a nice fall. Last week we had two days in a row where the wind was under fifty miles per hour, and everyone's calves are weighing pretty good. Our calves are the biggest ever which is sure a surprise considering the short grass and scant water.

I have an idea that may help my fellow cattlemen and me out of this situation of low product prices and ever higher input costs. It would be something like the dairy herd buy-out program but with a special twist. Not only would we get the federal government to buy all our lower producing cattle, but they could also pay us not to raise beef - we'd call it the **C**attlemen's **R**elief **P**rogram.

The possibilities here are endless. These could be deficiency payments if the prices go too low, and federally subsidized calf crop insurance; just think of all the new government jobs that will open up because of this. There could be special clauses so you would still get paid even if you started raising buffalo or elk as an alternative crop. Call me crazy, but it has happened in other industries and had great success.

We had a case of that mad cow disease last week. A cow of ours had hoof rot so I roped her out in the pasture and gave her a super-sized injection of antibiotics. In all those western movies you always see those cowboys roping big angry Longhorns, but you never see any of those guys getting their ropes off. Well, there's a good reason. It's a lot easier to rope something than to unrope something.

Like our famous western artist Charlie Russell said, "Ropes are just as dangerous as guns. The only difference is guns go off and ropes go on."

This age-old problem confronted me last week. A method that has shown marginal success in the past is to fashion the dallies of the rope into a slip knot and release the animal by simultaneously pulling the long tail of your rope and removing the loop. I call this *The Hail Mary method of cow releasing*. Now for my young readers out there, never try this at home. This is a process appropriate only for highly trained professionals or expendable cowboys.

My story begins as I was at the critical moment of the Hail Mary cow release. Instead of continuing to pull back, the cow charged ahead, as if she intended to retain the rope and some of my other cowboy gear as some type of memento of the event. This problem was compounded by the fact that I was still wearing my chaps while she was trying to put them on. The only thing I accomplished by pulling the slipknot off my saddle horn was to turn my faithful horse, Benny, loose. He's never been one to back you up in a fight, anyway, and he must have been late for the barn because that's where he went.

So here I am with this freshly injected cow straddling me, and I had a great opportunity to see her hateful eyes. Then it all started coming back to me. Every year when we trail our cows to a pasture on the river, this cow and her calf duck in the thick brush on the way. She stays in her dark haunt all summer, only coming out occasionally at dusk to maul some poor unsuspecting fisherman or meet with other cows of the same sinister nature. They probably sit around eating loco weed while watching bull riding videos and planning on how to break into hay corrals or instigate a stampede. I should have given this cow a shot a long time ago - right between the eyes.

This was a cow I'd bought from a neighbor, John Rumney - the same one that had suffered a uterine prolapse and I'd sewn up that very sensitive area without any pain medication. If you can imagine someone using a shoelace-sized cord to effect a drawstring type arrangement on your pucker muscle, then you can relate to the gratitude this cow experienced for this opportunity.

You can bet this cow had been waiting for a moment like this for a long time, I noticed her eyes brighten, and it was the first time I ever saw a cow smile. She looked at me like a sinner looks at a honky-tonk and proceeded to coat me with cow snot from one end to another. This is exactly why we cowboys wore six-guns. It wasn't for show-downs at high noon or robbing stage lines. They were used to defend themselves against crazed longhorns or to dispatch their horse if they were being dragged to death. I went for my weapon and, of course, I didn't have anything more lethal in my pocket than my cell phone.

Luckily just then I remembered an old Indian sayin': **"If you have short arms, don't wear your guns low."**

Like most old Indian sayings it didn't do me much good. Thank heavens for cell phones. I thought as I jabbed and poked at the cow's nose with the tiny antenna. Because I was experiencing limited success and it was getting on in the day, I opted to break the cardinal rule of cowboys everywhere. I decided to call for help and attempted to dial 911. This was sure no easy process with the cow still molesting me and all.

Someone answered with a Jamaican accent. "Hello mon—ya got Big Ruby at de lovers Psychic Help Line."

"I--need--(groan) help!" I shouted. "I'm in big trouble (gasp). On the range, a big cow (grunt), an Angus, is squashing me."

" Ohh, I be tuned in, mon. Big Ruby sees all. I sense dere be plenty a pain dere. You feel like your girlfriend Agnes is smothering you, and now she's breaking your heart. Am I right, mon?"

"Actually there is lots of pain, but the part she's breaking is a little lower than that, and it's an Angus not Agnes. She's a cow!"

"You have a girlfriend named Angus?"

"I'm a cowboy, and it's not a girlfriend-I'm married."

"I knowed ya was a cowboy 'cause I could here ya doin dat yodellin stuff. Now Big Ruby says ya doan do no more weird stuff wid dat fellow Angus, mon, and you quit callin' your wife a big cow, an' maybe she quit dat slammin' you on da stove."

About that time I lost cell service. I had gotten one leg loose and started kicking the cow in the nose. Since she'd already had her way with me, and given me a good case of range rash, she went back to her calf. I could see the whole activity had agreed with her as she sprightly moved off with hardly a limp.

I carefully got up and examined myself. I had dirt in every orifice and I was sticky all over. She had, at one point, gotten a hoof in my pants pocket and my new straw hat looked like one of those hats an English sea captain would wear, with the front and back of the brim bent straight up to the crown. It's hard to look like you're on your last legs when you just walked two miles home and you're not bleeding anywhere, but I did my best.

My wife snorted and raised an eyebrow at my appearance.

"You look like a glazed doughnut, and your hat's on sideways," she said.

I gave her an account of my near-death experience and included every grisly detail. My voice quavered throughout the story and trailed off weakly at the end.

"Jeez, I thought you might be worried when you saw my horse come back or even have heard me yellin'," I whined.

"Well, I'll be. I did hear all that ruckus, but I thought it was either the coyotes howling at the dogs or maybe an Indian attack."

I could see she was gravely concerned, but she stolidly concealed her emotions with a feigned hearty laugh and some coarse instructions.

"Well, get those sticky clothes off and don't be tracking any dirt in here."

She then went to the phone while humming one of her favorite tunes, "Short People Got No Problems". I assumed she was calling a paramedic or Mercy Flight. Instead it was her mother.

"You know what the old cow whisperer did now?" she asked her mom.

Holly relays, approximately the cow carnage story over the phone, and then her mom must have told a joke to try to cheer her up, because Holly's bent over laughing, and I can hear her mom laughing over the phone.

When Holly hangs up the phone, she has tears in her eyes, and I know she won't be able to keep up her brave front much longer so I left her alone to work out her emotions.

CHAPTER EIGHT

Cooking at the Ranch

*T*he annual sweetheart breakfast at our church was a big success. I was unable to attend because the morning of the breakfast I became nauseous and dizzy. It may have been the pressure of everyone's high expectations of my contribution to the breakfast. Our parish was hoping for some of my famed Tater Tot Surprise, but instead I had elected to make beer batter pancakes from scratch. A neighbor who ranches up the road, Frank Crabtree, brought a green bean dish that was quite a hit. The folks who were in attendance have told me over and over and over how good it was.

Frankly, Frank, I'm a little sick and tired of hearing about your prowess as a chef. He lucks out with one casserole and suddenly he's the Julia Child of Mission Road. I'll let you in on a little secret - you open a couple cans of green beans and some cans of cream of mushroom soup - duhh - like that's rocket science. Get a clue!

I'll have you know I'm nobody's fool when it comes to culinary expertise! Once when I ordered the deluxe Ginsue knife set, it came with a complimentary guide and instructional video to Oriental cooking - Benihana style. I learned how to slice, dice, and make Julianne fries in a flash, while reciting martial arts screams. I was very dedicated and religiously went to the basement to practice in secret. I had one setback on lesson seven, "Samurai Sausages", when during a particularly difficult exercise sequence I lost my grip on the knife and nearly neutered the cat. The layers of Band-Aids on my fingers did impede my dexterity somewhat. Still I felt confident I could surprise my family with my new talents at the first opportunity.

As good luck would have it we had an infestation of mice in the basement that fall. My wife dismissed my loud antics downstairs believing I was once again having difficulty attempting to set and adjust all the spring-loaded mouse traps, or most probably, was in the downstairs bathroom battling the consequences of some free government cheese that I had overindulged in. All was going according to my perfect plan.

Thanksgiving Day, my wife's entire family arrives. Guess who's asked to carve the turkey? I can hardly contain myself, and right after the blessing I start with my best yell and whack that turkey right in the ol' giblets, my seven-inch cleaver working in graceful unison with a big carving knife. Holly's mom screamed and grabbed her crystal dish full of fruit salad. Then, in her haste to vacate the festivities, she achieved a degree of speed and elevation that enabled her to tear the spring off the screen door and mow down the top of her beehive hairdo simultaneously as she darted outside.

Her seventy-six-year-old auntie, Violet, vaulted across the table at me, and I had to poke her with the baster a couple times to get her to settle down. The family all made a big deal out of it and constantly gave me dirty looks throughout the meal. They sat around there frowning and gumming that turkey like a bunch of cows chewin' cheat grass. I mean, gee, people pick bones out of fish, why not stuffing?

This is a recipe you may want to clip and save. I learned how to do this during my seven years as a college student. It's pretty technical so I'll talk you through it as I make some.

Beer Batter Pancakes from Scratch

Ingredients
One six pack of quality beer
One of them little sacks of Krusteaz instant
pancake mix

First - using discretion, sample one of the beers to make sure it hasn't gone bad.

Second - in a mixing bowl dump in pancake mix stirring in beer until it is about the consistency of fresh calf scours. Then dispose of the rest of the beer in an appropriate manner as to avoid waste and spillage.

Third - have some beer to ward off possible dehydration.

Fourth - in a pre-heated, greased skillet pour in dollops of the batter.

While you're waitin' you might as well have another beer. Just wait 'til old Crank Frabtree gets a load of this. He'll be yesterday's news. Have another beer- it's probably on the house - literally. When the bubbles in your babber buddle all the way uf, plip your fancakes. Are they good - who cares - just don't burn yourself and when you're outta beer, you're done cookin'.

CHAPTER NINE

The Day Jerome Saved Pike

About 12 years ago I worked on the 71 Ranch up by Martinsdale, Montana. It's a big beautiful cattle ranch that's part of the land that Wellington D. Rankin put together.

Jerome, one of the cowboys that worked there, loathed another one whose name was Pike. This Pike character was from Kansas City, and a wannabe buckaroo, and he never found a cow the whole time I knew him.

It was in the fall, and we were gathering the country around Forest Lake to get the cattle ready to ship. We usually spent a little more than a week finding most of the cattle up there and then we'd let Jack Frost gather the rest. The standard procedure was - we'd trailer our horses up the main drainage, then scatter out and gather all the cattle we could find, throw 'em down-country, and then they'd start trailing home. The only way out of there, other than the down main road, was to ride over the top of a sizable mountain ridge.

We were supposed to be back to the trailer with all the cattle we found by three in the afternoon. Pike never was. We'd look for cattle all day and Pike all night. He had absolutely no common sense, couldn't remember that water ran down hill, and always had some fantastic excuse as to why he was usually found going the wrong way without any cattle. There is a saying "having him around is worse than having two good men gone." This sure applied to Pike, and a centrifuged chicken would have a better sense of direction. His sorry performance affected the whole outfit. It's always been considered bad form to bitch to the boss about someone in the crew so we just tried to put up with him.

If you were trailing cattle down the road, it took Pike an extra half-hour to get dressed. He had fancy spurs, big high-topped boots with his pants tucked inside, a wild rag, and a great big black hat. The rest of us secretly hoped one of the high winds in that country would hit that hat and either blow him back to where he was from or rip his head off. He took himself very seriously, and as

I can see by your outfit...

you might imagine, was not very popular with the other cowboys, especially Jerome.

On that place we were to shoe our own string of horses and Pike didn't know how. Our boss, Errol Galt, told Jerome to teach Pike. When I heard this, I knew there would be trouble so I made a point to be in attendance. Jerome was just like a little bear - short but very stout. Jerome gave

110% to what ever he did, and he was a little chargie for my taste, but always good help. Jerome had a beard that covered his whole face and neck. All you could see under his big hat was his bright eyes and the end of his little button nose. If you can imagine an Ewok in a "Hoss" hat, you can envision Jerome.

One last critical fact for your understanding of these events is that before Pike decided to be a buckaroo, he was going to be a karate expert. Now you have an adequate knowledge of the characters for the story of "The Day Jerome Saved Pike".

*J*erome is showing Pike how to nail on a horse-shoe, and even though he'd been shown the right way, Pike starts the nail inside out. Jerome patiently explained the error to Pike, then things got weird. Pike drops the horse's foot and he later told me he was so upset with himself that he had to go into his "khata". What this involves is a series of thirteen different martial arts moves where you snap your arms around and hiss and sneer.

Pike says it gets you all calmed down and focused. Well, neither Jerome, I, nor the horse had ever seen one before, and Jerome jumped to the conclusion that Pike's having an epileptic fit.

When Jerome was in high school some 20 years before (back in North Dakota), he had been credited with saving a classmate's life during gym. Some young man had a seizure, and it was said Jerome had kept him from swallowing his tongue and choking. This must have been a high point in Jerome's life, because he jumped right into action trying to get a hold of Pike's tongue with his stubby little gloved fingers.

Pike, who had always been justifiably suspicious of Jerome's motives, resisted vigorously.

So here's these two guys rolling through the horse turds, Jerome trying to get his fingers in Pike's mouth, and Pike snapping and spitting like a mad badger. In the heat of the moment, I think Jerome forgot his original intention was to save Pike's life and just let the situation carry him away.

Well, finally Pike got loose and ran to the bunkhouse, and Jerome must have figured he'd sufficiently saved him because he quit chasing him at the barn door. I talked to them both afterwards and that's how I found out about Jerome's previous heroics in high-school, Pike's karate days and what a "khata" is, otherwise it would have just been written off as two cowboys gone postal.

Our church out on Mission Road is going to have a special Christmas service this Saturday night and everyone is welcome. This church is a quaint little log building way up in the mountains. It was built in 1865 when Montana was still a territory and the Jesuits came out to Christianize the Indians. The evening really gets you in the Christmas spirit and we have a get-together here at the ranch afterwards.

Proverbs 18:9

CHAPTER TEN

Honesty

*L*ast week I had a chance to contemplate honesty. This all started when my frowning wife was shuffling bowlegged down the hall and snapped, "Did you use the last of the toilet paper?"

My survival instinct kicked in, and I started thinking of options. Option one, luckily there are small children in my home that lacked the verbal skills to defend themselves against unjust charges. Regrettable collateral damage, but better than me taking the fall.

I can't lie to save myself, but I do enjoy some latitude with the truth. I needed to stall.

"Me?" I gasped.

"Ya, you, you little twerp," she sneered.

"Little twerp" is her favorite recent nickname for me.

Still stalling, I distinctly remembered the empty cardboard roll that I had ravaged that morning. Some of my tater tot surprise had erupted a volatile reaction on my delicate system, and I had not yet taken the time to get more paper and reload the little holder dealie.

Thinking quickly, I reasoned, the cardboard roll was there, cardboard is a member of the paper family, so technically---

"No I did not use the last of the paper! I can't believe you think I'm capable of such a thing." I replied indignantly.

It was after this I got to thinking about little white lies, fibs, stretching the truth, or "Clintonizing."

I surmised that St. Peter might be a little more lenient about some transgressions than others. For instance, how about keeping perfect score on cash income for your thrifty partner the I.R.S. Many of my friends in college thought they were completely exempt from the truth when it came to asking girls to dance with 'em or go out on a date. Girls tell even worse lies to get out of those engagements. I know that one time an attractive young lady somehow got the idea I was a wealthy talent scout for a modeling agency. I'd go into this full detail, but Father Hruska from our Church reads this column and he's only so understanding.

I think the truth is most abused when it comes to sins of flatulence. I can assure you in my house, when an offensive odor is called into question, confessing works nothing like it did for George Washington and the ol' cherry tree incident. I go with the same theory that good defense attorneys use - always plead innocent. Your punishment is no worse even if you're found guilty. So what's the upside to coming clean?

Here are a few prerequisites for the successful denial of an odiforous indiscretion:

There must be at least three mammals present at the scene. Being able to cast doubt on another is imperative.

There can be no audible sounds emanating from your posterior. It's impossible to evade responsibility if you sound like an Evinrude boat motor.

During my annual chili-eating binge, if I feel I might need an alibi, I keep my dog, Bernie, with me at all times. It's the only time I allow him in the cab of my truck.

Last summer, a blue-blooded yuppie couple, Princeton and Buffy, had engaged my services as a fly fishing guide. They were treating me to dinner and as they had flown in, we were to be going in my old ranch truck.

I own an extended cab pickup, and in the cab I keep stocked all of the technical equipment it takes to run a modern cattle operation. The important stuff, like ropes, bridles, wrenches and vet supplies, I keep in the front of the cab. These are neatly arranged and categorized on the dash, seat, and floor. The other gear I don't need as often such as empty beer cans, Chester Fried chicken wrappers, kids, feed sacks, and tax deductible receipts, go in the rear compartment.

Princeton and Buffy tentatively climbed in the front of my pickup, and I ordered my poor old dog Bernie to wade through the junk and get up on the small back seat.

Buffy seemed very interested in the various tools and devices around her as she positioned herself in the middle.

"What's this?" She had sat on a big shiny tubular device used for forcing big medicine boluses down cattle.

"A balling gun," I said.

"Eeuuu!" she exclaimed, smiling weakly as she dropped it like a dirty diaper.

"How about this?" Princeton asked as he held up a sticky orange clump.

"It's either polly twine or my calving chain from last spring," I offered.

Well, pretty soon I was sure glad I had my dog along because I was having one of those not so fresh feelings. Sometimes with intense concentration, and a dedicated sphincter, you can delay and even redirect bad gas back to its origin. I was attempting this process when Princeton asked. "Why are you driving with your eyes closed and your butt all the way off the seat?"

I didn't want to risk a breach in the air lock I had going, so I just nodded in agreement and stepped on the gas. Damn, I thought, all that bean dip I had at the Driftwood Bar might really hurt my chance for a big tip from these clients. Submitting to the inevitable, I sat down, relaxed, jerked my thumb toward the back seat and charged my dog with the offense.

"He does this all the time," I added, frowning and shaking my head for effect.

While I was cursing Bernie, I glanced around at my passengers to see how well my clever ruse had worked.

It wasn't pretty at all. Princeton was gagging with his head out in the wind. Buffy's eyes were shut tightly with her hand clamped over her mouth and nose. Sadly, she had opted for suffocation. The most damaging fact of all was that somehow Bernie had suspected something and had managed to frantically paw open the small camper window above the back seat. He had been riding in the bed of the truck the whole time.

Proverbs 19.5

74

CHAPTER ELEVEN

All Charlies Go to Heaven

Some of the neighbors went to Gene O'Neil's funeral Monday. I met Gene the second year we were here. A friend and I went up to look at some of his horses and we had a very interesting visit. He said his grandfather received some land here on Lepley Creek as a Civil War pension, and that's how they got started in this country.

Dennis Harris is well into calving, and the Lanes' heifers are just about to start. Kelsey England had her 6th birthday party last Saturday. Our five-year-old son was going to attend, but he had pink eye, and Dr. Patton (the vet) glued a patch over it so he was too embarrassed to go.

Anyone who's had young children knows how much story books or videos shape their thoughts. Our son Jake had watched the movie "All Dogs Go To Heaven", where the hero is a dog named Charlie; so when he got a puppy, that was his name.

Jake loved Charlie and they were together all the time. Charlie was killed by a truck when he was about a year old, and, of course, Jake was devastated, so we got a new puppy immediately. Jake named this dog C.D. that stood for Charlie Dog. Jake and C.D. got along fine and all seemed well.

One day about a week before Christmas Jake said, "You know what I want for Christmas?"

"What?" I asked.

"No, I mean, what I really want?" he said.

"What?" I asked again. I love him so much I'd get him anything within reason, and since he's the family cowboy I figured he'd want new pistols or a saddle or something like that.

"I want a long rope, a really, really long one. I can throw it way up in the clouds and Charlie can bite it, and I'll pull him back down to me."

Well, talk about a lump in your throat. Adding to the trauma his new dog C.D. developed seizures and had to be put to sleep. We got a new puppy right away to try to soften his loss. Of course, Jake named him Charlie.

Jake didn't really seem that upset about C.D.'s demise, and one day about a month after we got the new "Charlie" Jake said, "You know, Dad, when this dog dies, I'm gonna name the next one Clifford."

It never ceases to amaze me how well my children have adapted to some of the relationships and interactions with the various animals we encounter on our ranch. I can just hear them recalling fond childhood memories.

"Ya, I had a kitten but the owl in the barn ate her and the coyotes killed Matt's dog. I raised a calf named Blossom, and one day my dad shot her and that winter we ate her. Oh, did I tell you about our household bats?"

Our house is 90 years old and every summer somehow a few bats sneak in. At first we found this quite unsettling and the event elicited screams, yells and hiding under the covers. The sadistic furry little kamikazes really seemed to enjoy this and scared the hell out of us on a regular basis. Having no previous bat-fighting experience, we were at quite a disadvantage, and our feeble attempts at bat extraction consisted of evacuating the premises and leaving lots of windows and doors open. We never knew how or where they squeaked in so we might come under surprise attack at any time. The term "sleeping with one eye open" fit us to a tee.

One late fitful night my wife suddenly announced, "There's a bat in the bed."

I can attest this statement captures your entire focus, and rate it as one of the world's best lines to get some sleepy head out of the sack. We instantly levitated and shot out the room at approximately the speed of light. Safely outside, we peeked back into the darkened room to see it. In between where we had been lying, just below the pillows, there it was on its back, wings spread out, and probably bat snoring. In any event it appeared to be sleeping a lot better than we had been.

When you turn on the lights it really excites these little vermin. I'm a half a head shorter but a beer belly wider so hero-like I stood in front of Holly and made ready for the onslaught. First I thought I should clear the air between Holly and me in case the next events took an ugly turn.

"Honey, I never really posed for any Soloflex ads like I said when we were dating, and you're some of the best damn help pairin' up cattle that I ever had."

Heart pounding and poised for battle I flipped on the light switch. It was Holly's hair bow innocently lying where it had come out.

We still have bats living in the attic and sometimes they sneak in the house, but we just don't get that excited about it anymore. When their flapping, scratching and squeaking get too loud during one of their little bat parties Holly just pounds on the ceiling and yells at them to quiet down. As if they were unruly up-stairs tenants or naughty kids. This seems to make them settle down and we have a new sort of symbiotic relationship. The friends of the earth would be proud of us. Now when one gets into the house the family is quite nonchalant.

"Daaad, there's another bat in the house" with no more excitement than telling me that the trash can is full or a light bulb needs changing. I, however, treat it as a breach of my defense perimeter and look upon it as an act of war. My method of extraction has changed dramatically and I actually embrace the opportunity to do battle with the little scumbags.

It gives me a chance to don my bat combat ensemble that includes:

A heavy canvas Carhart coat
    – for the flack jacket effect

A good hat
    – gives me some head protection and I
    always feel more courageous with
    my cowboy hat on.

Chaps and welding gloves
  – self-explanatory

Sports safety glasses
  – in case they try any dirty little bat tricks
  like spitting in my face when I get
  'em cornered

A wild gleam in my eye
  – self-explanatory

And finally, my premium piece of bat combat gear, my ultra secret weapon, the bane of bats all over the county

My racquetball racquet
  – Old Reliable.

I wear it slung low on my hip in quick draw fashion and swagger around the house. With an attitude. Their little bat radar can't detect the strings. Stealth-mode bat engagement. I like it.

"Feelin' lucky, you little hairball? Wanna meet God, bug eater? Just come on in to the ol' bat motel. Meet Mister Racquet and make my day."

My wife Holly believes this whole bat thing has played into my alleged Napoleon complex. I admit I have been entertaining some detailed thoughts of making a siege and strategizing on how to retake the attic.

Genesis 1:26

CHAPTER TWELVE

Errol's Wild Ride

We had a real good hunting season. We do some outfitting and our hunters killed some nice big bull elk and some dandy mule deer bucks. We all saw lots of mountain lion tracks this year. One of my guides and his hunter saw a big cat and I saw a fresh kill. Jim Cornelius used his nice new Belgian team and wagon to take a hunting camp into the Bear Tooth Game Range and I guess they really worked well.

Right after my cowboying job on the 71 Ranch down by Martinsdale, Montana, I took a job in an office in Great Falls. I was an errand boy and a secretary for my cousin, Rick. I hated the job and found it very confining, but my dad, after repeated attempts, had finally convinced me I'd never get anywhere or achieve anything working on a ranch. This all happened about 16 years ago, and it was probably one of the biggest favors my dad ever did me.

My former ranch boss was a nice fellow named Errol Galt, and we were good friends. Errol and his wife, Sherry, had come over Christmas shopping and she had left him off with me in the early afternoon and I was supposed to have him at his sister's house south of town for a nice dinner at 8:00 sharp.

Well, there was a little bar downstairs in the building where I worked, and we went down there to visit and have a couple beers. Time really got away from us and pretty soon it was 8:30 and we were sure late. We jumped in my pickup and started hurrying out there on this gravel road going to his sister's place. We were speeding along and I remember I was telling some story about riding a bucking horse or something and I ran square off the road. It was pretty steep right there so I didn't dare try getting right back on the road just then, and I could see what looked like a little better spot in my headlights down country a ways. I could also see that I was sure going to need some momentum, so I didn't let off the gas one bit. This all happened during a key moment of the story I was telling, and I never quit talking, driving, or waving my arms around.

I was looking over at Errol about this time and he was leaning way back in the seat, his arms were stiff at his sides, his eyes were great big and his mouth was sagging open. At the time, I just figured he was anxiously awaiting the next line in my story, a reaction I had experienced many times, so I didn't give it much thought. I got out of the ditch okay, and when we got to his sister's house, we weren't even quite stopped and he was outta the truck. I attributed his hasty exit to the fact we were a bit tardy and dismissed any concern.

As it turned out, I never saw Errol for a long time afterwards and even now our only contact is an occasional Christmas card that his wife, Sherry, sends. I sure miss all our good times but you know how it is when we all get so busy.

A friend of mine was driving to Cut Bank up on the route they call the High Line a few years ago. It is huge open country. He saw a beat-up old car approaching that was being pursued by a tribal policeman with his siren and lights on. The fleeing car was really going fast and completely missed a sharp curve in the road between them. The car flipped-end-over end out into a plowed field and threw the driver out on the ground. My friend and the policeman got to this curve at about the same time and went running out to the field to see if the guy was alright. When they got out there, the fellow had managed to get up to his knees but was pretty woosy.

The first thing the policeman asked the guy, "Are you ok?"

"I yi think so," the guy answered, reeking of alcohol.

"Are you drunk?" the officer then asked.

Through bleary eyes the driver looked quizzically up at the officer and said. "Of course, I'm drunk. Whaadaya think, I'm a shittin' stunt driver?"

Now that I'm older I don't drive as fast, walk as fast, heal as fast, etc. Every day it takes me a little time to get the kinks out, and I descend the stairs like an old saddle horse walks down hill. When a cow gets to be about ten years old, she is usually missing some teeth and we refer to her as a broken mouth. She usually starts lookin' sorta' poor and is not long for the world. Most of these cows have joints that click when they walk and they take short, little halting steps. When one of these cows goes by us in the sorting alley in the fall, we say she's doin' the Packin' House Shuffle. My friends would say I'm getting kinda "shelly" myself, and I'm not going to betray my age but my dentist would say I must be over ten cow-years old. In the mornings I gimp into the kitchen to gum down my breakfast in a manner that impersonates Quasi Moto after hip surgery.

I need lots of vitamin pills, mineral pills, aspirin tablets to keep my blood thin, and some Ibuprofin to get limbered up. To save time I just dump 'em in a bowl, pour in some milk and sugar and I'm ready to go.

CHAPTER THIRTEEN

Marketing

Very often my friends ask me, "How do you do it? You seem to be semi-retired at a young age; you have a great-looking wife and family. What is your secret?"

It wasn't always this way. My financial statement was so weak it didn't even have a pulse, and the only feminine attention I ever received was on my monthly therapy session at the Tokyo House of Massage, Feed Store, and Casino.

Then I discovered the importance of marketing. I started by going to the dance halls and honkeytonks, where I would slip into the unoccupied girl's bathroom and scratch on the walls - FOR A GOOOD TIME CALL SKIP - and leave my current phone number.

Also, I made use of the singles column:
SINGLE WHITE MALE, TALL, ATHLETIC,
FINANCIALLY SECURE, SEEKS LUSCIOUS
BABE WHOSE DAD HAS ELK HUNTING AND
HORSE PASTURE ON HIS RANCH.

If you want to get any apples, you have to shake a few trees.

What I can't stand is when people misuse advertising by misrepresenting the facts or wasting the public's time and attention. Or what about these realtors who have their faces all over the paper. I think it's safe to say that most of us are much more interested in a photo of the property than one of the real estate agent. A lot of times it's some questionable-looking person with a seductive smug smile on their face, like they might be willing to meet you in some lounge if you make them an offer on their current listing.

When I owned my small brokerage company, I studied demographics and marketing a lot to get the most from my advertising budget. I read this article in the *Harvard Business Review* entitled "Marketing Myopia" (July-August 1993).

In essence, this story related how a lot of big businesses missed the mark by not capitalizing on the full scope of their product. The article uses the petroleum industry as an example. It turns out some of their best and most profitable byproducts, such as plastics and pharmaceuticals, were ignored for years, and all the industry wanted to focus on was selling fuel. The theme of the story evolved as to the fact that it took the industry an inordinate amount of time to realize that they needed to sell a whole line of petroleum-related products. There is a fortune to be made along this line of thinking, the "mother" of all marketing strategies. I'm pretty busy with calving right now so I'm going to pass along a couple of my million-dollar ideas so some of my readership can take one and run with it.

NAUGHTY GIRLS' PSYCHIC HOT LINE

This one would make a killing because you could capture the entire market share. You could charge a little more because people could get their sick thrills and ambiguous generalized fortune told at the same time. It would go something like this:

Caller: "Is this the naughty girls' psychic hot line?"

"O h h, b a b y, y e s, i t i s. I w a n t t o c h a d y o u r d i m p l e, a n d I h a v e t h e f e e l i n g y o u 're a b o u t t o g e t s c r e w e d o u t o f t e n d o l l a r s a m i n u t e."

Here's another little gem.

ODOR EATERS-- ALTERNATIVE USES

Dr. Scholl is really missing the boat on this one. All he needs to do is fashion a little adhesive and he'd make a killing. Picture this - an odor eater hanging from the rear view mirror as an air freshener. Or how handy it would be to stick them in your underwear and have an odor/vapor barrier with a simultaneous muffling device. You could then sell em' to tree huggers to re-tread their Birkenstocks. Yes, friends the key to your success, too, is marketing.

CHAPTER FOURTEEN

Labor Pains

*L*ast week when I was out one night checking the cows I tried to make a mental list of all of the advantages of calving when it's 26 degrees below zero. Understandably, it was a pretty short list. About the only thing I could come up with was that the calving chains don't slip out of your hands because they freeze right to your fingers when you're tryin' to snare a leg.

I remembered how worthless our childbirth classes were that Holly required me to attend at our own children's births. I went to a couple of the classes and then I wanted to quit. I already had a very good understanding of the mechanics of the process and besides the scheduled time-slot conflicted with happy hour at the Angus Bar. I'm hell on finishin' something once I start though, so I went all the way through.

I'll tell you we cowboys could show those obstreperous obstetricians a few things that would really get these health care costs down and the process speeded up. For one thing, in place of an hourly wage, those folks should get paid by the head. Then instead of acting like a bunch of cheer-leaders at a chess match they'd behave more like someone who doesn't want to miss too much late night TV.

I mean I stayed all the way through when our second son, Matthew, was born and it was quite an inefficient process. I didn't see any type of familiar equipment there, and I think the whole town paraded through there at one point or another gazin' and gabbin' like it was some kind of social event.

"Sure, come on in, that's my pretty wife over there with her feet in the air. Want some coffee or cookies?"

Holly was yellin' so much I had to keep turning up the volume on the TV, and the whole deal was very unsettling. When Matthew finally popped out, he looked just like that boxing promoter, Don King, after he had been slimed.

Then the doctor asks, "Do you want to cut the umbilical cord?"

And I think, "I'm not licensed for this, and what the hell are we payin' you for if I'm gonna do everything?"

Even when we got home, things didn't get much better. He pooped all day and cried all night. When Holly got up to feed him, sometimes she joggled the bed and it was tough for me to get a full night of sleep. It had been a difficult pregnancy. Holly was extra sensitive and didn't appreciate anything I did for her.

She said she needed some maternity clothes so I bought her some new Carhart bibs with the expando button sides. She said they made her look "hippy." Next she complained that all of the extra outside work was drying out her skin and making her old before her time.

"Hell, you just had a hot oil massage last week," I said.

"Getting sprayed by a broken hydraulic line on the tractor is not the same," she pouted.

For her cattle feeding duties I bought her a round-bale un-roller. I timed this with her birthday so she wouldn't have to handle all those little square bales anymore - and actually she did tear up and get a bit emotional over that one.

It didn't get that much easier when Matthew got older either. He and all his whiny little friends wanted to have an Easter egg hunt.

"Help yourself," I said. It was time to gather the eggs anyway. "You'll probably have the best luck lookin' under the hens in the chicken coop. Have fun, and don't come crying to me if you get pecked."

For his fifth birthday he wanted me to demonstrate how to play Pin the Tail on the Donkey. What a stupid game, and here's a little safety tip - never, ever, use a real mule.

CHAPTER FIFTEEN

The Rancher's Rodeo

*F*rank and Bobbi Crabtree told me about a good five- year-old gelding they have for sale, he's a nice quiet bay that Chuck had been heading steers off over at Augusta.

Art Dupuis and Rosemary Semens both called last week to let us know about a church service at the Mission, Saturday, July seventh.

Everyone out here has started cutting their hay and it is not too bad of crop so far. It's been awfully dry and smoky. We don't like to see the cut hay get rained on, but the country could sure use the moisture.

Jim Cornelius and Mary had a birthday party for Barb Eschenbacher last Friday evening, where a humorous misunderstanding took place and caused Barb to drop her walker. Evidently the batteries in her hearing aid were low and when we all shouted "BLOW ON THE CANDLES", she thought we said - "Let go of the handles". No permanent harm was done as Barb is pretty spry for thirty-two and she jumped right up and ate most of the cake.

It was sure good to see so many Cascade residents participating in the United Way Ranchers Rodeo in Great Falls. The event raised more than $4,000 for United Way, and there were 43 rancher teams.

The Steinbachs from Augusta were the overall champs, and many Cascade contestants made a strong showing. The three events in the Rodeo were team branding, team penning, that Jill Lane's team won, and finally the ribbon roping. This last event required three team members and emphasized family participation. It's mandatory that there be at least one senior citizen and one female. Usually she runs the ribbon back to the starting line and the other members rope or mug the calf. Our team consisted of myself, Holly, and my elderly uncle.

I had hoped to ride Buck. He's experienced, reads cattle, and is pretty fast for a short distance. At the last minute I decided not to use him after the old bugger tried to kick me. He had recently developed a bad attitude when I had to use my spurs or quirt to encourage him. Also, the front cinch of my saddle was really chafing him under his armpits and his bifocals kept steaming up.

As the ladies raced back, many of the spectators and other contestants would yell and voice cheers of support to the runners - a great display of sportsmanship and good will. One local rascal, Bobby Lemire, the foreman of the Dana ranch, was a blatant heckler throughout the day and he especially enjoyed a small social blunder that occurred during the last event.

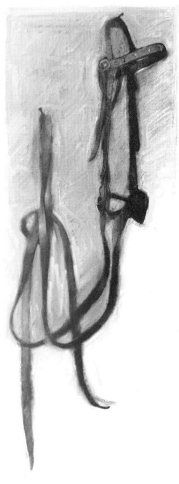

This was only a minor incident but it put a blemish on the otherwise sterling day.

It started when an overzealous cowboy thought he detected the initial symptoms of a heart attack as Jill Lane wheezed across the finish line. He immediately pounced on her and began C.P.R.

In Jill's defense, she resisted bravely and fought me off in no time at all. I'd like to report that the little altercation was quickly laughed off, but, in fact, it turned into one of those embarrassing social situations where the lady tried to give me electro-shock therapy with a cattle prod.

I went down to the Stockgrowers' Convention in Billings last winter and that was sure fun. Several ranchers from the Cascade area were down. I ran into Collin

Murnion down there and we had a nice visit. Collin has a ranch down by Jordan, and he was in the lead going into the National Finals in the bareback riding a few years ago.

A while back I was staying overnight with Collin and he told me a funny story about a neighbor. This particular neighbor drank a lot of whiskey and the authorities had seen fit to remove him from his drivers license, so he had to either have his wife, Peach, drive him or he rode his horse. This was years ago when Collin and his brothers were very young and this fellow used to stop by their place to visit and brag about his good quiet horse on the way home from the bar.

One day Peach was on her way home from getting groceries and spotted her husband's horse tied up at Collin's folks' place and stopped. This fellow convinced every one he could just lead his horse into the back of the old ranch pick-up to haul him home - no stock rack or anything - and just sit on the end gate and hold the lead rope of his horse. Well, when Peach eased out of the ditch where they had loaded the horse, she slipped the clutch too much and killed the engine. This guy sittin' on the end gate is showin' off, and hollers at his wife about how she ought to know better and that she was a sorry driver and finishes his tirade by yellin,' "Now, dammit, wind 'er up, Peach."

Well, Peach revs up the truck and drops the clutch.

The horse pops out the back of the truck, and avoided serious injury only because his fall was broken by the guy holding the lead rope. They end up hauling this fellow to the hospital and Collin says the next time they see him ridin' by he ain't stoppin' and he has enough gauze on his head to build a turban. From then on whenever he's goin' by they all yell, "Wind 'er up, Peach."

Chapter Sixteen

Alaskan Adventure With Bert

*H*olly and I have been getting ready for our platoon of hunters. We've been scrubbing cabins and chasing the mice out and getting our horses ridden down. I've noticed our two main dude horses, Terminator and Powder Keg, are a little fresh this fall.

My father-in-law, Bert, and I went to Alaska fishing, and I shot a caribou. We flew into Anchorage, then Dillingham, then went by boat to Mission Lodge at Aleknagik.

We saw moose at the Guilapac, grizzlies on the Togiak, and caribou at Kulakak. I developed a theory that they name these places by getting you airsick on the float-plane, then the first sound that emanates from your body when you land is what they name that lake or river.

I'm proud to say that they named Lake Upachuk after me.

The fishing was fantastic! We caught lots of Rainbow Trout, Arctic Char, Arctic Grayling, and huge Silver Salmon.

 We got along great with our Indian fishing guides. We were very honored that they christened us with native names. They called Bert "Elcheapo" and me, "Slapsthewater".

I found caribou hunting a bit overrated. A pilot flew another fellow and me way off to a lake on a huge expansive tundra with our camp gear. "Be back here with all of your meat day after tomorrow." That was our complete list of instructions, guidelines, and precautions. Neither one of us had ever hunted caribou, and to say the least, we were a bit intimidated by the remote location. It did not help that we saw a grizzly bear the size of a buffalo the first morning out.

Envision shooting two yearling, grass-fat steers, cutting them up into five handy eighty pound loads, and then backpacking them two and one-half miles through a swamp while fighting bugs. My caribou looked an awful lot like Prancer, so Santa might be one short on the wheel team. If that's the case, I'm probably positioned on the big list somewhere between the bottom of who's naughty and the top of sh_t!

Bert and I have very different fishing styles. I use mostly dry flies with a tiny leader and a six-weight rod. He prefers trolling with worms and cowbells on line that you could use to rope calves.

I was landing a nice Rainbow on a shallow stretch of the Gilapac River. We were anchored in a small boat, and my fish became tangled in some sticks near the shore. Bert stepped out of the boat and waded over to the fish with our large landing net in hand. He was just approaching the trout when a HUGE, BROWN GRIZZLY stepped out of the brush twenty yards upstream from him. This happened to be this bear's private stretch of fishing beach and Bert couldn't have looked guiltier. Imagine catching a fox in the hen house with a bird in his mouth. The bear looked at Bert like a fat man looks at the last piece of pizza.

As I always do in such situations, I thought of others first. At great personal risk I courageously tried to distract the bear by making repeated quick splashing and paddling motions with the boat oars. I thought it might throw the bear off-guard to see a drift boat achieve a plane and dash up the river without the benefit of a motor. When the guide restrained me, I grabbed our video camera hoping to get some snappy action footage of a sixty-six-year-old man out-running a mad bear.

I've always aspired to be a wildlife photographer, and this was just like a scene from my favorite childhood TV program, *Mutual of Omaha's Wild Kingdom*. I loved that show and Jim Fowler was my hero. The Crocodile Hunter would have crapped his khakis if he had tried some of the stuff Jim pulled off. Marlin Perkins was the senior part of the duo and he would wait at the top of the cliff, or the edge of the swamp, in the jeep, etc. Meanwhile, Jim would be over the cliff, in the swamp, trying frantically to save himself by catching up to the jeep, etc. The director who set up the wildlife encounters obviously had a sense of humor and probably later became the driving coach for "Vince and Larry." The director also probably had a big life insurance policy on Jim, and Homer Simpson could have come up with better capture strategies.

Since Jim usually had his hands full Marlin would do the narrating.

"I'm here in Dumbambi by the famous Lagoon of Death. I'll be monitoring the fuel gauge on the Land Rover while we are attempting to determine the constricting capability of a full-grown male, giant water anaconda. Our plan, it seems, is to let the monstrous reptile wrap itself around Jim as many times as possible and I should be able to determine the pressure by how far his eyes bug out. It's times like these he can take great comfort in knowing he is protected by life insurance from Mutual of Omaha. I always hoped Jim would get a gut full of the deal and revolt.

"Dammit, Marlin, I got the last two. This time I'll hold the horses and you go up in the tree and get the throat culture. Besides I'm allergic to cats. Especially large enraged ones with big teeth who kill deer for a living."

"Remember, Jim, I contribute to your 401k and I also have film of you kissing that yak."

But I digress. Back to the matter at hand and my own video. My father-in-law Bert was hogging all the good action scenes and had already snapped up the role of Jim Fowler, so I was left with the part of Marlin Perkins.

Following is the narrative of my excellent home movie:

"Bert and I are in the wilds of Alaska trying to enrage savage animals for some abstract reason that will hopefully motivate you to purchase life insurance. I'll stay here and supervise the boat motor while my associate deals with large hairy predators along the shore."

"There is something moving in the bushes," I proclaim excitedly. "Why, it's a huge ugly carnivore, the Grizzly Bear. *Ursus horriblus* is the Latin name, and these bears are very defensive of their territory. They can tear off a moose's head with one swipe or out run a quarter horse. Watch out! That bear looks mad, and those claws are razor sharp!" I caution. "Here he comes now, *spouse's fatherus speedius.*"

The panting, wild-eyed beast charged across the water straight at the boat...meanwhile the bear was nonchalantly munching on salmon up the river.

Since Bert, thinking only of himself, dropped his roll as Jim Fowler and attempted instead to emulate a track-star in hip waders, the last scene really suffers with a weak ending. My wife always thought her dad could walk on water; little did I know.

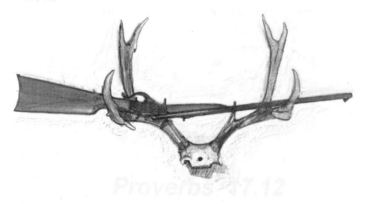

CHAPTER SEVENTEEN

S.O.L

My sister, a rural mail carrier, asked Sunday how our P.M.R. was.

"What's a P.M.R.?" I asked.

"Postmaster Relief," she said.

I got to thinking a person could have a lot of fun with these abbreviations. Like - what if your P.M.R. got P.M.S.? You'd be S. O. L. Reminds me of when I was dating Holly. I'd go park and try to administer a little C.P.R. out in the C.R.P. If she got P.O.'d, there could be a T.K.O.

Now on a more serious note I had the opportunity to pay my fair share to the I.R.S. last Monday. The only thing that eased the pain at all was the comforting knowledge that my hard earned dollars were being prudently spent on such valuable activities as million dollar plane trips for Hillary Clinton, wolf reintroduction, and ferret studies.

It seems I had underestimated my quarterly estimates. Somehow I had gotten my schedule B's mixed up with my 1099 B's and the net result was a very nasty tax consequence. I had been expecting a healthy refund this year, so you can imagine my disappointment when our accountant informed me that instead I had to come up with a bunch of money. It didn't seem like we had made much money last year, with the low calf prices and all, but my accountant said I'd frittered all our money away on milk, diapers and an occasional generic beer.

I now believe my accountant to be a secret I.R.S. agent who works on a commission, and the whole experience rated right up there with throwing dead calves in the coulee.

The first winter we were married we were as poor as a couple of crows. My mom lived with this widow woman who sold us a washer and dryer out of her summer cabin for $35 for the pair. Holly was very skeptical right from the start, but I wasn't about to let a deal like this go.

I told Holly, "Opportunity knocks but doesn't break the door down," so I bought 'em sight unseen.

"The last time opportunity knocked and you bought something sight unseen was when you blew all our savings on that hunting dog with the pedigree you just couldn't live without," Holly said.

"That dog has a hell of a lot a heart and can pick up a two-day-old scent."

"I remember the whole pathetic story," she continued. "You were going to make a killing raising registered hunting dogs. When we drove up to the Indian reservation to pick her up, that old guy told you *she has good nose, but she don't look so good*. 'She looks just fine to me,' you said and couldn't give him our money fast enough," she whined.

"Well, she is of excellent bloodlines and can really smell birds. We'll just see who's the smart one someday, Mrs. Nelly Negative, when it's considered the ultimate in sportsmanship to use a bird dog that's blind."

"Well, excuuuuse me, if I'm less than thrilled. It's just that we're still strapped from when you maxed out our credit card on that cubic zirconium investment package you got sucked into off of that TV infomercial."

Well anyway, it was my first major appliance purchase and I was pretty excited -- until I saw 'em. First off they looked like some kinda Buck Rogers reject deal. The corners were all rounded off, the washer didn't work and the dryer smelled like it was the hang-out for a bunch of incontinent mice.

The washer had about 12 colored buttons across the top, every button for a different laundry problem. They ranged from the hot pink "soiled cotton" button on the far left all the way to the lime green "oily polyester" on the far right. These things were ready for the Washing Machine Hall of Fame, but I hauled 'em home anyway.

The dryer worked pretty good; you had to jamb a spoon in the door to keep it shut, but two hours later you had some damp clothes that smelled like mouse pee.

That washer, however, gave us fits right from the start. You'd hit one of those colored buttons and the thing would start clickin' and snappin' getting all geared up for the job; it would then fill up with water and immediately flood the house. When I got that fixed, I found out about the "extra scrubber action" feature it touted in the parchment owner's manual that the lady had thrown in with it. The big stem deal in the middle of the tub had these obscene black spiny appendages on the top and they would wind all your clothes up and leave permanent dark greasy marks on 'em.

This winding up of the clothes feature also got the machine out of balance, and it would come pounding away from the wall like a crazed beast, tethered only by the hoses.

Holly was still in college then and studied constantly. The hallway of our trailer house that the washer was in was narrow enough, and her legs long enough that she sat and studied her books on the washer and held it in place by bracing her legs across the hall. I tried my best to sit on it a couple of times, but I'm so short it didn't work out. My feeble attempts at confining that machine from hell would have reminded you of a drunken rodeo rider. Besides, my spurs were scratching the enamel and the whole process made my beer foam up.

One night we had asked our friend, Dave Dear, for dinner and when the thing went into the wind-up-and-pound cycle, Dave's eyes started getting big. We tried to act nonchalant, as if we weren't surprised at all that someone might be using a jack hammer in our back hallway. Next the thing fought all the way out to the kitchen and then dumped its water like a slurry bomber fighting fire, and Dave asked, "Does it wax the floors, too?"

A little while later I made the lady give me my $35 back and Holly's been soured on used appliances ever since.

CHAPTER EIGHTEEN

Frank's Flat Toe

My family and I are members of the Sacred Heart Parish here in Cascade. We always sit by Frank and Bobbie Crabtree because we like them and they help us watch our kids. It seems like Frank and Bobbie are really grateful for our company too, because the minute they see us enter the church they hit their knees and duck way down in silent prayer.

Between stand up, sit down, kneel and singing while wrestling our kids it's a great workout. The last time we went, there was a reading - Paul to the Phillippinoes, I think. I don't remember what Paul said, but he should have included "for heavens sake don't ever elect a female president named Imelda with an obsession for shoes. She'll break your country."

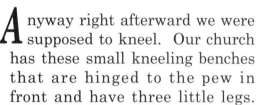

A nyway right afterward we were supposed to kneel. Our church has these small kneeling benches that are hinged to the pew in front and have three little legs. Well, my kids love playing with it, and whipped that thing down right on poor Frank's toe, and then before he could extract it, the whole pew crushed it down while kneeling. Frank was right beside me, and he was fanning his hands around, with his mouth open but no sound was coming out. He then, for the first time since puberty, captured all the high notes in "Amazing Grace", and went on to do a fair rendition of Lee-Ann Rimes crooning the "Lonesome Cattle Call."

Well, fortunately for once, it was a short prayer. I believe it was something about when Sampson smote the Hutterites, and we all sat back down so Frank could get his sore flat toe out of harm's way. Frank was explaining to me what happened as he limped out of the church, and I was right behind him as Father Hruska shook our hands in greeting as we left. A puzzled look came over the Father's face as Frank flicked a tear out of his eye, then a look of satisfaction and he quickly looked around to see if his sermon had the same effect on the rest of the congregation.

I know it's the time of year when we're supposed to turn our thoughts toward spiritual growth and pray for good will and such. What I usually ask for when I pray is that my wife will become more like that girl Daisy on the old TV show the "Dukes of Hazard". Now I'm not thinking only of her outstanding physical attributes or her keen sense of fashion. What I really liked about her is she would shut up and let a man drive. Remember Bo or Luke would be racing towards a big wash-out or some other dangerous obstacle with the law hot on their heels. If they got to the river and the bridge was gone, no problem, they would just use the bank or the old washed out frame as a take off ramp and fly right over. All this time you never heard a peep out of Daisy. What a woman! She probably has her own fat trust fund and owns a brewery besides.

To demonstrate what a contrast my own situation is, I'll tell you what happened last week. We were on our way home in our "family wagon" and I was driving. It seemed like everyone was sleeping so I started playing the old Montana driving game "squash the gopher".

I was pretty hot that day and luckily most of the gophers were on my side of the road. When I went for my eighth confirmed kill, I had to hang a couple wheels down in the ditch. Well, that shoulder of the road was pretty soft, so pretty soon I had all four wheels down in the ditch. Holly picked this untimely moment to wake up, and immediately jumps to the conclusion that our bouncing up the ditch in her new Ford Explorer is somehow my fault. In the brief time it took me to regain the road she called me names that would have made a sailor blush and put knots on my head big enough for a calf to suck on.

CHAPTER NINETEEN

Thinking Too Much

*M*y first job, besides working for my dad on the cattle ranch I grew up on, was guiding and packing for my brother-in-law. He was an outfitter in the Scape Goat Wilderness area. He had a hunting camp way up on the Continental Divide that he got snowed out of early every year, so the U.S. Forest Service allowed him another camp that was lower, and only three miles in from the end of the road or "trailhead."

It was towards the end of the season and there had been a good herd of elk up on the ridge west of our camp. We could see from their tracks that they had fed down into the bottom of a drainage and made plans to roust them out. My part in this plan was to take a couple of hunters up on the adjacent ridge and distribute them, with instructions to go to the bottom of the drainage and then go up the creek. I told them I would be waiting with the horses and other hunters at the head end. We all met at the rendezvous point except the elk, of course, and the first hunter I had dropped off. I waited the rest of the day; and when he didn't show up, I hoped he had made his way back to camp on his own. When you're a guide and you lose your hunter, it looks real bad. My boss sent the other guide and me out immediately to track him down. This involves riding through downfall with a flashlight on a steep mountain sidehill without the benefit of a dinner. I was very worried; I felt responsible and was trying to come up with every possible scenario that could explain the situation and help us find the hunter.

The other guide, Bear, is a lot older and more experienced than I am, besides being a lot bigger and meaner, so I'm very willing to listen to his advice, instruction and abuse. He wasn't too happy to be spending his "damned slight and well-earned sleeping time" tracking down my hunter. Of course, we find his tracks right away and we see where he turned down the drainage at the bottom instead of up. I guess water runs up-hill wherever he was from. We track him down the creek for a ways until he travels all the way out of the wilderness and hits a logging road. We later see where he is picked up by a vehicle. We are riding back towards the trailhead and it really hasn't taken that long or been that bad, so our spirit and attitude are starting to improve. We were pretty sure the guy is okay wherever he is, so Bear suggests we drive in to Lincoln to "have a little warmer-upper." I'm in no position to argue, and besides our boss will figure we're out scouring the mountains for his client so what's the harm?

We were just walking into the Wilderness Bar and who should be there but our hunter. He is very surprised and happy to see us and tells us so. We tell him about how the problem originated when he went the wrong direction at the creek bottom. He said he figured that out about the time he hit the logging road but was afraid to start back into the wilderness so late, so he caught a ride to town. On his way to town a herd of elk crossed the road, he had killed a fair bull, and it was already in the local meat locker. He then voiced his amazement at how we had found him.

Bear doesn't miss a beat and says, "You were a little tough to track when you got in that truck, but I always get my man."

This incident during my formative years had a profound effect on my attitude toward life. I realized that despite minimal effort and very weak discernment on our part in this situation, everything worked out great. I surmised that in my short life I'd been trying too hard and thinking too much. I had never liked thinking anyway and me instructing myself to relax and not to think too much was like asking a pyromaniac to sit down by the fire. I was a nineteen-year-old cowboy and bull-rider at the time, and my brain cells were all waving little white flags surrendering to head concussions and excesses at beer stands. I had also recently finished reading the works of a famous French philosopher, Jean Paul Descartes, who was remembered for the ridiculous quote, "I think, therefore I am."

This, mistakenly, led me to my own personal presumption, "I am awake and breathing, so therefore I must be thinking."

Obviously, other people share my theory not to think too much. Otherwise there wouldn't be so many examples of enacted ideas that just seem "wrong." Like Bob Dole selling Viagra, dancing bears at the circus, Pee-Wee Herman, painful and strange body piercing, etc.

When forced to really concentrate on a subject, like college level calculus, I realized right away that IT HURTS TO THINK, so I'd stop immediately. Sometimes thinking would sneak up on me and I'd catch myself in deep contemplation, so I would quickly distract myself with television or music. Occasionally, when an intense episode of the thought process is distracting me I have to read, watch TV, listen to the radio, and talk on the phone simultaneously in order to avoid focused concentration.

Ideally I would keep my mind completely uncluttered with lots of R.A.M. available on my hard-drive. In case there is an emergency and I need to think, I don't want anything in the way. I make a mental note to immediately discard from my mind any phone numbers and long personal names, etc., so it won't clog up my memory banks. People like me are born to delegate responsibility.

Having all this extra brain capacity available gives me immense self-satisfaction. It's like having a great book on the shelf or a six-pack of good beer in the fridge. A lot of the pleasure is in knowing it's there when I want it. I have developed a grand capacity for worthless information, like the names of movie stars or authors, but have no recall what-so-ever of important daily facts or events, such as which day I turned the bulls in with the cows. So, consequently, I'm a great trivia partner, but I have no idea when we'll start calving.

Not everyone, especially my wife, Holly, agrees with my theories on thinking and capacity for memory. Where I consider my mind seasoned and introspective, she thinks it's pickled from too much cheap beer and watching "X-Files" re-runs. Actually, my memory is excellent...it's just not very long.

Proverbs 3:5

CHAPTER TWENTY

Hunting Season

We had a real good season. Our hunters killed some nice bull elk and mulie bucks. It would have to be characterized as the year of dangerous guide tricks. The first one, we laughingly referred to as "Guides Flambeau."

One of our best guides, George, wanted to give his hunters a hot lunch, so he stopped into the Butte Creek cabin. This structure is an old cowboy line shack near the top of Elk Ridge that we sometimes camp in during hunting season. George, our wrangler, and two clients were hunting up there around noon and decided to eat their lunch in the cabin. At this point, the event is best described according to the accident report filed by the Worker's Compensation caseworker.

"Subject received minor burns, cuts and contusions from an incident on Oct. 28th at approximately 12:15 p.m. The victim appears to be almost completely recovered, other than a general trembling of voice and panicked demeanor that seems to be responding well to increased dosages of Thorazine."

"The incident was apparently accidental, contrary to the suspicions of the preliminary report. Even though the guide's wages and working requirements are deplorable, this was evidently not a staged overly dramatized statement of protest as is practiced in some Far Eastern cultures. Following is the order of events proceeding and causing the injuries as surmised from interviews with two guests and a co-worker."

"Victim allegedly poured copious amounts of Coleman lantern fuel on kindling in the cabin stove. The third match ignited the wood in stove, fuel can in victim's hand, gloves, coat, and especially the hat of victim. Victim abandoned the 'Stop, Drop & Roll Method', and instead elected and attempted to immerse himself in nearby creek. Victim hastened through door, did several brief pirouettes, fended off co-worker who was attempting to subdue the flaming garments with a shovel, gave brief chase to co-worker, then proceeded to creek with great urgency. The creek is unfortunately, only six inches wide and two inches deep near the cabin so the immersion attempt required a systematic turn and spin process much like the classic crocodile death roll."

Signed,

Ken Nethstarr
Special Investigator
Bureau of Worker's Compensation
Questionable Claims Division

Don't think for a minute that my Worker's Comp rates aren't going up after this deal. What that the accident report omitted is that when the fuel can ignited, George dropped it, and set the whole cabin on fire. He shouted to Justin (the horse wrangler), "SAVE SOMETHING!"

Justin is only seventeen, and with wisdom surpassing his years, he abandons the precious camping gear, the expensive hunting equipment, and instantly chooses an out-dated stack of Playboy magazines that some degenerate cowboy on his way back from Snediker Basin had left there.

A life-threatening event like this really pulls the crew together, though, and all the other guides voiced lots of concern and support.

"George, I was watching the Discovery Channel and they had a show about guys like you, 'Spontaneous Human Combustion'."

"Hey, Zippo. Do you feel any better since you quit smoking?"

You can see why we outfitters pay such huge insurance premiums. Because of incidents such as the above, I've felt it would be handy to start a list of outfitters commandments:

Thou shalt not start fires with lantern gas.

I think my next one would be -

Thou shalt leave all the guts up on the mountain.

This whole liver thing ticks me off. For years growing up, when I had to clean up my plate, at some point during the year, usually during hunting season, I had to eat liver. Moms in those days had this theory that if something tasted really bad, it was "good for you." Well now, come to find out it's not good for you at all. It has all the benefits of movie popcorn with cholesterol sauce.

How come these idiots had to wait until I was of age to find that out? The whole idea of eating weird animal parts is outdated in my opinion. Now, if it was 100 years ago and I was stranded on Donner's Pass in January, I might lower my standards. If the situation necessitated me to eat tongue, heart, tripe, head-cheese, blood sausage, brain fritters, liver and the rest of that stuff, starvation wouldn't seem like such a bad option.

"This liver's real good fried up in bacon grease with onions," my dad would say. "Ooh boy, hold me back and pass the catsup, both bottles."

My thoughts are, you could probably mince up cat lips, season, sauté, and cook em' and you could choke them down too, but in a world where you can buy two Tony's Pizzas for $5 why in the hell would you?

I have eaten a lot of Rocky Mountain oysters, better known to most of us as calf nuts, in my day. But I only did it because all the older ranch kids practiced the tradition, so I knew it must be in vogue. This is the same peer pressure that started me chewing tobacco, cursing, riding bulls, and some of my other more enviable attributes.

When I was older, I continued so no one would question my loyalties or sexual preferences. In Montana if you pass up a meal of deep fried calf nuts you might just as well have a "WE LOVE WOLVES" bumper sticker or march in a gay rights parade. Since I'm already branded as having Democrats for relatives, and I'm a sometimes Mr. Mom, I eat em' every time they're offered.

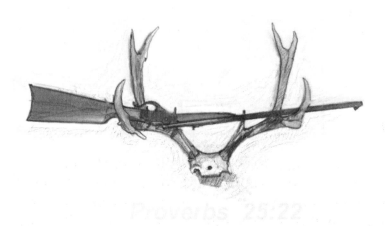

CHAPTER TWENTY-ONE

Misery

I know I haven't written for awhile, but events have taken a bitter turn out here on the Lepley Creek Ranch. The origins of these problems probably started a long time ago but have only come to an ugly head as of late.

I guess my wife, Holly, had been feeling a bit overwhelmed. She's the mother of three small children, a coach for the youth basketball team, our laundry service, a nurse at the hospital, and the efficient housekeeper of our old farm house.

As usual, Holly's mother planted the seeds of our discontent. This happened one Sunday afternoon early this spring. Holly had prepared a nice dinner, cleaned and shined the house and all the rest of us, in anticipation of her parents' visit. I had been planning to clean up my horse shoeing tools all week and had a little time to kill before the dinner, so I brought in my shoeing box and proceeded to meticulously work them over in the kitchen sink.

I was just getting a good start when Holly's folks arrived, and she came downstairs to greet them. Right away Holly sternly started in on me.

"Gosh, honey, I wish you would have waited until after dinner to clean those. The horse poop sometimes clogs the drain."

Holly's mom has always felt I married far above my station, physically and socially. She consistently takes Holly's side and refers to me as "Hagar the Horrible," and just the mention of my name causes her blood pressure and her eyebrows to elevate dangerously. She consoles Holly, and I find out later that she encouraged her to go to an assertiveness training workshop that she was sponsoring.

This alone would probably not have upset my peaceful existence had it not coincided with Holly's new workout routine. She consistently gets up about five in the morning to do an aerobics tape or go walking.

One morning when she was finished and woke me with my morning coffee in hand, she said, "I'm getting bored with these aerobic tapes and would like to try something different."

Well, as bad luck would have it, just then on TV there was this professional trainer/promoter selling his new workout video. This video which absolutely has ruined my life involves the combination of aerobics, dancing, and Kick-boxing--the dreaded TAE-BO.

Even now I shake, and my voice breaks just saying the words, but bravely, I will relay the sequence of events that has led to my miserable recent existence.

One muddy day early this spring the kids and I came in from cleaning the barn and happened to forget to take our overshoes off when we waltzed into the kitchen on her newly mopped floor. When she sees all the muddy tracks, and only a quarter of 'em are mine, remember, she says, "I just cleaned and waxed this floor!"

I've always been known for my witty comebacks and say, "Well, good. That means your mop bucket is still handy." This brought a good laugh from me and a chuckle from the kids.

KERBLAM! All of a sudden my eyes were watering, my nose running, and my ears ringing. It happened so fast I didn't even see it and had to get the details from my boys. They are real fans of martial arts movies and were able to describe how she used moves and distributed blows that would have put a Ninja to shame.

Well, now when she asks us to wipe our feet, or pick up our own messes, you can bet your sweet keaster we hop right to it, and I live in abject terror of her next PMS episode.

By golly, things are going to have to change around here, and I'm going to take a stand - just as soon as I'm done cleaning the bathrooms, and she's done watching her movie --- starring Jackie Chan.

TO ORDER COPIES OF
THE COW WHISPERER

Please send me _____copies at $$9.95 each plus $2.00
shipping and handling.
(Make checks payable to Quixote Press)

Name _____

Address _____

City _____State_____Zip_____

CALL 1-800-571-2665
QUIXOTE PRESS
1854 - 345th Ave
Wever, Iowa 52658

Please send me _____copies at $$9.95 each plus $2.00
shipping and handling.
(Make checks payable to Quixote Press)

Name _____

Address _____

City _____State_____Zip_____

CALL 1-800-571-2665
QUIXOTE PRESS
1854 - 345th Ave
Wever, Iowa 52658

Since you have enjoyed this book, perhaps you would be interested in some of these others from **QUIXOTE PRESS**.

ARKANSAS BOOKS

ARKANSAS' ROADKILL COOKBOOK
        by Bruce Carlson . . . . .paperback $7.95
REVENGE OF ROADKILL
        by Bruce Carlson . . . . .paperback $7.95
LET'S US GO DOWN TO THE RIVER 'N...
        by Various Authors . . . . .paperback $9.95
TALL TALES OF THE MISSISSIPPI RIVER
        by Dan Titus .paperback $9.95
LOST & BURIED TREASURE OF THE MISSISSIPPI RIVER
        by Netha Bell & Gary Scholl . . . . .paperback $9.95
TALES OF HACKETT'S CREEK
        by Dan Titus .paperback $9.95
101 WAYS TO USE A DEAD RIVER FLY
        by Bruce Carlson . . . . .paperback $7.95
VACANT LOT, SCHOOL YARD & BACK ALLEY GAMES
        by Various Authors . . . . .paperback $9.95
HOW TO TALK MIDWESTERN
        by Robert Thomas . . . . .paperback $7.95
ARKANSAS COOKIN'
        by Bruce Carlson . . . .(3x5) paperback $5.95

DAKOTA BOOKS

HOW TO TALK DAKOTA . . . . .paperback $7.95
Some Pretty Tame, but Kinda Funny Stories About Early
DAKOTA LADIES-OF-THE-EVENING
        by Bruce Carlson . . . . .paperback $9.95
SOUTH DAKOTA ROADKILL COOKBOOK
        by Bruce Carlson . . . . .paperback $7.95

REVENGE OF ROADKILL
>by Bruce Carlson ....paperback $7.95
101 WAYS TO USE A DEAD RIVER FLY
>by Bruce Carlson ....paperback $7.95
LET'S US GO DOWN TO THE RIVER 'N...
>by Various Authors ....paperback $9.95
LOST & BURIED TREASURE OF THE MISSOURI RIVER
>by Netha Bell ....paperback $9.95
MAKIN' DO IN SOUTH DAKOTA
>by Various Authors ....paperback $9.95
THE DAKOTAS' VANSHING OUTHOUSE
>by Bruce Carlson ....paperback $9.95
VACANT LOT, SCHOOL YARD & BACK ALLEY GAMES
>by Various Authors ....paperback $9.95
HOW TO TALK MIDWESTERN
>by Robert Thomas ....paperback $7.95
DAKOTA COOKIN'
>by Bruce Carlson ....(3x5) paperback $5.95

ILLINOIS BOOKS

ILLINOIS COOKIN'
>by Bruce Carlson ....(3x5) paperback $5.95
THE VANISHING OUTHOUSE OF ILLINOIS
>by Bruce Carlson ....paperback $9.95
A FIELD GUIDE TO ILLINOIS' CRITTERS
>by Bruce Carlson ....paperback $7.95
Some Pretty Tame, but Kinda Funny Stories About Early
ILLINOIS LADIES-OF-THE-EVENING
>by Bruce Carlson ....paperback $9.95

ILLINOIS' ROADKILL COOKBOOK
by Bruce Carlson . . . . .paperback $7.95
101 WAYS TO USE A DEAD RIVER FLY
by Bruce Carlson . . . . .paperback $7.95
HOW TO TALK ILLINOIS
by Netha Bell . . . . .paperback $7.95
TALL TALES OF THE MISSISSIPPI RIVER
by Dan Titus .paperback $9.95
TALES OF HACKETT'S CREEK
by Dan Titus .paperback $9.95
LOST & BURIED TREASURE OF THE MISSISSIPPI RIVER
by Netha Bell & Gary Scholl . . . . .paperback $9.95
STRANGE FOLKS ALONG THE MISSISSIPPI
by Pat Wallace . . . . .paperback $9.95
LET'S US GO DOWN TO THE RIVER 'N...
by Various Authors . . . . .paperback $9.95
MISSISSIPPI RIVER PO' FOLK
by Pat Wallace . . . . .paperback $9.95
GHOSTS OF THE MISSISSIPPI RIVER
(from Keokuk to St. Louis)
by Bruce Carlson . . . . .paperback $9.95
GHOSTS OF THE MISSISSIPPI RIVER
(from Dubuque to Keokuk)
by Bruce Carlson . . . . .paperback $9.95
MAKIN' DO IN ILLINOIS
by Various Authors . . . . .paperback $9.95
MY VERY FIRST
by Various Authors . . . . .paperback $9.95
VACANT LOT, SCHOOL YARD & BACK ALLEY GAMES
by Various Authors . . . . .paperback $9.95
HOW TO TALK MIDWESTERN
by Robert Thomas . . . . .paperback $7.95

INDIANA BOOKS

REVENGE OF ROADKILL
      by Bruce Carlson ....paperback $7.95
LET'S US GO DOWN TO THE RIVER 'N...
      by Various Authors ....paperback $9.95
101 WAYS TO USE A DEAD RIVER FLY
      by Bruce Carlson ....paperback $7.95
VACANT LOT, SCHOOL YARD & BACK ALLEY GAMES
      by Various Authors ....paperback $9.95
HOW TO TALK MIDWESTERN
      by Robert Thomas ....paperback $7.95
INDIANA PRAIRIE SKIRTS
      by Bev Faaborg & Lois Brinkman .....paperback $9.95
INDIANA COOKIN'
      by Bruce Carlson ....(3x5) paperback $5.95

IOWA BOOKS

IOWA COOKIN'
      by Bruce Carlson ....(3x5) paperback $5.95
IOWA'S ROADKILL COOKBOOK
      by Bruce Carlson ....paperback $7.95
REVENGE OF ROADKILL
      by Bruce Carlson ....paperback $7.95
GHOSTS OF THE AMANA COLONIES
      by Lori Erickson ....paperback $9.95
GHOSTS OF THE IOWA GREAT LAKES
      by Bruce Carlson ....paperback $9.95
GHOSTS OF THE MISSISSIPPI RIVER
(from Dubuque to Keokuk)
      by Bruce Carlson ....paperback $9.95

GHOSTS OF THE MISSISSIPPI RIVER
(from Minneapolis to Dubuque)
        by Bruce Carlson ....paperback $9.95
GHOSTS OF POLK COUNTY, IOWA
        by Tom Welch ....paperback $9.95
TALES OF HACKETT'S CREEK
        by Dan Titus ....paperback $9.95
TALL TALES OF THE MISSISSIPPI RIVER
        by Dan Titus ....paperback $9.95
101 WAYS TO USE A DEAD RIVER FLY
        by Bruce Carlson ....paperback $7.95
LET'S US GO DOWN TO THE RIVER 'N...
        by Various Authors ....paperback $9.95
TRICKS WE PLAYED IN IOWA
        by Various Authors ....paperback $9.95
IOWA, THE LAND BETWEEN THE VOWELS
(farm boy stories from the early 1900s)
        by Bruce Carlson ....paperback $9.95
LOST & BURIED TREASURE OF THE MISSISSIPPI RIVER
        by Netha Bell & Gary Scholl ....paperback $9.95
Some Pretty Tame, but Kinda Funny Stories About Early
IOWA LADIES-OF-THE-EVENING
        by Bruce Carlson ....paperback $9.95
THE VANISHING OUTHOUSE OF IOWA
        by Bruce Carlson ....paperback $9.95
IOWA'S EARLY HOME REMEDIES
        by 26 Students at Wapello Elem. School ..paperback $9.95
IOWA - A JOURNEY IN A PROMISED LAND
        by Kathy Yoder ....paperback $16.95
LOST & BURIED TREASURE OF THE MISSOURI RIVER
        by Netha Bell ....paperback $9.95
FIELD GUIDE TO IOWA'S CRITTERS
        by Bruce Carlson ....paperback $7.95
OLD IOWA HOUSES, YOUNG LOVES
        by Bruce Carlson ....paperback $9.95

SKUNK RIVER ANTHOLOGY
          by Gene Olson .paperback $9.95
VACANT LOT, SCHOOL YARD & BACK ALLEY GAMES
          by Various Authors . . . . .paperback $9.95
HOW TO TALK MIDWESTERN
          by Robert Thomas . . . . .paperback $7.95

KANSAS BOOKS

HOW TO TALK KANSAS . . . . .paperback $7.95
STOPOVER IN KANSAS
          by Jon McAlpin . . . . .paperback $9.95
LET'S US GO DOWN TO THE RIVER 'N...
          by Various Authors . . . . .paperback $9.95
LOST & BURIED TREASURE OF THE MISSOURI RIVER
          by Netha Bell .paperback $9.95
101 WAYS TO USE A DEAD RIVER FLY
          by Bruce Carlson . . . . .paperback $7.95
VACANT LOT, SCHOOL YARD & BACK ALLEY GAMES
          by Various Authors . . . . .paperback $9.95
HOW TO TALK MIDWESTERN
          by Robert Thomas . . . . .paperback $7.95

KENTUCKY BOOKS

TALES OF HACKETT'S CREEK
          by Dan Titus . . . . .paperback $9.95
LOST & BURIED TREASURE OF THE MISSISSIPPI RIVER
          by Netha Bell & Gary Scholl . . . . .paperback $9.95
LET'S US GO DOWN TO THE RIVER 'N...
          by Various Authors . . . . .paperback $9.95

101 WAYS TO USE A DEAD RIVER FLY
by Bruce Carlson . . . . .paperback $7.95
TALL TALES OF THE MISSISSIPPI RIVER
by Dan Titus .paperback $9.95
MY VERY FIRST
by Various Authors . . . . .paperback $9.95
VACANT LOT, SCHOOL YARD & BACK ALLEY GAMES
by Various Authors . . . . .paperback $9.95

MICHIGAN BOOKS

MICHIGAN COOKIN'
by Bruce Carlson . . . . .paperback $7.95
MICHIGAN'S ROADKILL COOKBOOK
by Bruce Carlson . . . . .paperback $7.95
MICHIGAN'S VANISHING OUTHOUSE
by Bruce Carlson . . . . .paperback $9.95

MINNESOTA BOOKS

MINNESOTA'S ROADKILL COOKBOOK
by Bruce Carlson . . . . .paperback $7.95
REVENGE OF ROADKILL
by Bruce Carlson . . . . .paperback $7.95
GHOSTS OF THE MISSISSIPPI RIVER
(from Minneapolis to Dubuque)
by Bruce Carlson . . . . .paperback $9.95
LAKES COUNTRY COOKBOOK
by Bruce Carlson . . . . .paperback $11.95

TALES OF HACKETT'S CREEK
    by Dan Titus . . . . .paperback $9.95
MINNESOTA'S VANISHING OUTHOUSE
    by Bruce Carlson . . . . .paperback $9.95
TALL TALES OF THE MISSISSIPPI RIVER
    by Dan Titus . . . . .paperback $9.95
Some Pretty Tame, but Kinda Funny Stories About Early
MINNESOTA LADIES-OF-THE-EVENING
    by Bruce Carlson . . . . .paperback $9.95
101 WAYS TO USE A DEAD RIVER FLY
    by Bruce Carlson . . . . .paperback $7.95
LOST & BURIED TEASURE OF THE MISSISSIPPI RIVER
    by Netha Bell & Gary Scholl . . . . .paperback $9.95
VACANT LOT, SCHOOL YARD & BACK ALLEY GAMES
    by Various Authors . . . . .paperback $9.95
HOW TO TALK MIDWESTERN
    by Robert Thomas . . . . .paperback $7.95
MINNESOTA COOKIN'
    by Bruce Carlson . . . .(3x5) paperback $5.95

MISSOURI BOOKS

MISSOURI COOKIN'
    by Bruce Carlson . . . .(3x5) paperback $5.95
MISSOURI'S ROADKILL COOKBOOK
    by Bruce Carlson . . . . .paperback $7.95
REVENGE OF THE ROADKILL
    by Bruce Carlson . . . . .paperback $7.95
LET'S US GO DOWN TO THE RIVER 'N...
    by Various Authors . . . . .paperback $9.95

LAKES COUNTRY COOKBOOK
by Bruce Carlson . . . . .paperback $11.95
101 WAYS TO USE A DEAD RIVER FLY
by Bruce Carlson . . . . .paperback $7.95
TALL TALES OF THE MISSISSIPPI RIVER
by Dan Titus .paperback $9.95
TALES OF HACKETT'S CREEK
by Dan Titus .paperback $9.95
STRANGE FOLKS ALONG THE MISSISSIPPI
by Pat Wallace . . . . .paperback $9.95
LOST AND BURIED TREASURE OF THE MISSOURI RIVER
by Netha Bell .paperback $9.95
HOW TO TALK MISSOURIAN
by Bruce Carlson . . . . .paperback $7.95
VACANT LOT, SCHOOL YARD & BACK ALLEY GAMES
by Various Authors . . . . .paperback $9.95
HOW TO TALK MIDWESTERN
by Robert Thomas . . . . .paperback $7.95
LOST & BURIED TREASURE OF THE MISSISSIPPI RIVER
by Netha Bell & Gary Scholl . . . . .paperback $9.95
MISSISSIPPI RIVER PO' FOLK
by Pat Wallace . . . . .paperback $9.95
Some Pretty Tame, but Kinda Funny Stories About Early
MISSOURI LADIES-OF-THE-EVENING
by Bruce Carlson . . . . .paperback $9.95
A FIELD GUIDE TO MISSOURI'S CRITTERS
by Bruce Carlson . . . . .paperback $7.95
EARLY MISSOURI HOME REMEDIES
by Various Authors . . . . .paperback $9.95
UNDERGROUND MISSOURI
by Bruce Carlson . . . . .paperpback $9.95
MISSISSIPPI RIVER COOKIN' BOOK
by Bruce Carlson . . . . .paperback $11.95

NEBRASKA BOOKS

LOST & BURIED TREASURE OF THE MISSOURI RIVER
  by Netha Bell .... .paperback $9.95
101 WAYS TO USE A DEAD RIVER FLY
  by Bruce Carlson .... .paperback $7.95
LET'S US GO DOWN TO THE RIVER 'N...
  by Various Authors .... .paperback $9.95
HOW TO TALK MIDWESTERN
  by Robert Thomas .... .paperback $7.95
VACANT LOT, SCHOOL YARD & BACK ALLEY GAMES
  by Various Authors .... .paperback $9.95

TENNESSEE BOOKS

TALES OF HACKETT'S CREEK
  by Dan Titus .... .paperback $9.95
TALL TALES OF THE MISSISSIPPI RIVER
  by Dan Titus .... .paperback $9.95
UNSOLVED MYSTERIES OF THE MISSISSIPPI
  by Netha Bell .... .paperback $9.95
LOST & BURIED TREASURE OF THE MISSISSIPPI RIVER
  by Netha Bell & Gary Scholl .... .paperback $9.95
LET'S US GO DOWN TO THE RIVER 'N...
  by Various Authors .... .paperback $9.95
101 WAYS TO USE A DEAD RIVER FLY
  by Bruce Carlson .... .paperback $7.95
VACANT LOT, SCHOOL YARD & BACK ALLEY GAMES
  by Various Authors .... .paperback $9.95

WISCONSIN

HOW TO TALK WISCONSIN . . . . .paperback $7.95
WISCONSIN COOKIN'
     by Bruce Carlson . . . .(3x5) paperback $5.95
WISCONSIN'S ROADKILL COOKBOOK
     by Bruce Carlson . . . . .paperback $7.95
REVENGE OF ROADKILL
     by Bruce Carlson . . . . .paperback $7.95
TALL TALES OF THE MISSISSIPPI RIVER
     by Dan Titus .paperback $9.95
LAKES COUNTRY COOKBOOK
     by Bruce Carlson . . . . .paperback $11.95
TALES OF HACKETT'S CREEK
     by Dan Titus .paperback $9.95
LET'S US GO DOWN TO THE RIVER 'N...
     by Various Authors . . . . .paperback $9.95
101 WAYS TO USE A DEAD RIVER FLY
     by Bruce Carlson . . . . .paperback $7.95
LOST & BURIED TREASURE OF THE MISSISSIPPI RIVER
     by Netha Bell & Gary Scholl . . . . .paperback $9.95
HOW TO TALK MIDWESTERN
     by Robert Thomas . . . . .paperback $7.95
VACANT LOT, SCHOOL YARD & BACK ALLEY GAMES
     by Various Authors . . . . .paperback $9.95
MY VERY FIRST
     by Various Authors . . . . .paperback $9.95
EARLY WISCONSIN HOME REMEDIES
     by Various Authors . . . . .paperback $9.95
THE VANISHING OUTHOUSE OF WISCONSIN
     by Bruce Carlson . . . . .paperback $9.95
GHOSTS OF DOOR COUNTY, WISCONSIN
     by Geri Rider .paperback $9.95

RIVER BOOKS

ON THE SHOULDERS OF A GIANT
     by M. Cody and D. Walker . . . . .paperback $9.95
SKUNK RIVER ANTHOLOGY
     by Gene "Will" Olson . . . . .paperback $9.95
JACK KING vs DETECTIVE MACKENZIE
     by Netha Bell .paperback $9.95
LOST & BURIED TREASURE OF THE MISSISSIPPI RIVER
     by Netha Bell & Gary Scholl . . . . .paperback $9.95
MISSISSIPPI RIVER PO' FOLK
     by Pat Wallace . . . . .paperback $9.95
STRANGE FOLKS ALONG THE MISSISSIPPI
     by Pat Wallace . . . . .paperback $9.95
TALES OF HACKETT'S CREEK
(1940s Mississippi River kids)
     by Dan Titus .paperback $9.95
101 WAYS TO USE A DEAD RIVER FLY
     by Bruce Carlson . . . . .paperback $7.95
LET'S US GO DOWN TO THE RIVER 'N...
     by Various Authors . . . . .paperback $9.95
LOST & BURIED TREASURE OF THE MISSOURI
     by Netha Bell .paperback $9.95
LIL' RED BOOK OF FISHING TIPS
     by Tom Hollatz . . . . .paperback $7.95

COOKBOOKS

THE BACK-TO-THE SUPPER TABLE COOKBOOK
     by Susie Babbington . . . . .paperback $11.95
THE COVERED BRIDGES COOKBOOK
     by Bruce Carlson . . . . .paperback $11.95
COUNTRY COOKING-RECIPES OF MY AMISH HERITAGE
     by Kathy Yoder . . . . .paperback $9.95
CIVIL WAR COOKIN', STORIES, 'N SUCH
     by Darlene Funkhouser . . . . .paperback $9.95

SOUTHERN HOMEMADE
      by Lorraine Lott . . . . .paperback $11.95
THE ORCHARD, BERRY PATCHES, AND GARDEN CKBK
      by Bruce Carlson . . . . .paperback $11.95
THE BODY SHOP COOKBOOK
      by Sherrill Wolff . . . . .paperback $14.95
CAMP COOKING COOKBOOK
      by Mary Ann Kerl . . . . .paperback $9.95
FARMERS' MARKET COOKBOOK
      by Bruce Carlson . . . . .paperback $9.95
HERBAL COOKERY
      by Dixie Stephen . . . . .paperback $9.95
MAD ABOUT GARLIC
      by Pat Reppert . . . . .paperback $9.95
BREADS! BREADS! BREADS!
      by Mary Ann Kerl . . . . .paperback $9.95
PUMPKIN PATCHES, PROVERBS & PIES
      by Cherie Reilly . . . . .paperback $9.95
ARIZONA COOKING
      by Barbara Soden . . . . .paperback $5.95
SOUTHWEST COOKING
      by Barbara Soden . . . . .paperback $5.95
EATIN' OHIO
      by Rus Pishnery . . . . .paperback $9.95
EATIN' ILLINOIS
      by Rus Pishnery . . . . .paperback $9.95
KENTUCKY COOKIN'
      by Marilyn Tucker Carlson . . . . .paperback $5.95
INDIANA COOKIN'
      by Bruce Carlson . . . . .paperback $5.95
KANSAS COOKIN'
      by Bruce Carlson . . . . .paperback $5.95

NEW JERSEY COOKING
by Bruce Carlson ....paperback $5.95
NEW MEXICO COOKING
by Barbara Soden ....paperback $5.95
NEW YORK COOKIN'
by Bruce Carlson ....paperback $5.95
OHIO COOKIN'
by Bruce Carlson ....paperback $5.95
PENNSYLVANIA COOKING
by Bruce Carlson ....paperback $5.95
AMISH-MENNONITE STRAWBERRY COOKBOOK
by Alta Kauffman ....paperback $5.95
APPLES! APPLES! APPLES!
by Melissa Mosley ....paperback $5.95
APPLES GALORE!!!
by Bruce Carlson ....paperback $5.95
BERRIES! BERRIES! BERRIES!
by Melissa Mosley ....paperback $5.95
BERRIES GALORE!!!
by Bruce Carlson ....paperback $5.95
CHERRIES! CHERRIES! CHERRIES!
by Marilyn Carlson ....paperback $5.95
CITRUS! CITRUS! CITRUS!
by Lisa Nafziger ....paperback $5.95
COOKING WITH CIDER
by Bruce Carlson ....paperback $5.95
COOKING WITH THINGS THAT GO BAA
by Bruce Carlson ....paperback $5.95
COOKING WITH THINGS THAT GO CLUCK
by Bruce Carlson ....paperback $5.95
COOKING WITH THINGS THAT GO MOO
by Bruce Carlson ....paperback $5.95
COOKING WITH THINGS THAT GO OINK
by Bruce Carlson ....paperback $5.95

GARLIC! GARLIC! GARLIC!

by Bruce Carlson ....paperback $5.95

KID COOKIN'

by Bev Faaborg ....paperback $5.95

THE KID'S GARDEN FUN BOOK

by Theresa McKeown ....paperback $5.95

KID'S PUMPKIN FUN BOOK

by J. Ballhagen ....paperback $5.95

NUTS! NUTS! NUTS!

by Melissa Mosley ....paperback $5.95

PEACHES! PEACHES! PEACHES!

by Melissa Mosley ....paperback $5.95

PUMPKINS! PUMPKINS! PUMPKINS!

by Melissa Mosley ....paperback $5.95

VEGGIE-FRUIT-NUT MUFFIN RECIPES

by Darlene Funkhouser ....paperback $5.95

WORKING GIRL COOKING

by Bruce Carlson ....paperback $5.95

SOME LIKE IT HOT!!!

by Barbara Soden ....paperback $5.95

HOW TO COOK SALSA

by Barbara Soden ....paperback $5.95

COOKING WITH FRESH HERBS

by Eleanor Wagner ....paperback $5.95

BUFFALO COOKING

by Momfeather ....paperback $5.95

NO STOVE-NO SHARP KNIFE KIDS NO-COOK COOKBOOK

by Timmy Denning ....paperback $9.95

MISCELLANEOUS

HALLOWEEN
       by Bruce Carlson ....paperback $9.95
VEGGIE TALK
       by Glynn Singleton ....paperback $6.95
WASHASHORE
       by Margaret Potter ....paperback $9.95
PRINCES AND TOADS
       by Dr. Sharon Tobler ....paperback $12.95
HOW SOON CAN YOU GET HERE, DOC?
       by David Wynia, DVM ....paperback $9.95
MY PAW WAS A GREAT DANE
       by R. E. Rasmussen, DVM ....paperback $14.95

To order any of these books
from Quixote Press
call
1-800-571-2665

About the Illustrator

R. Tom Gilleon

Tom lives on his ranch near Cascade, Montana where he is captain of the fencing team. He has worked as an illustrator for NASA, U.S. Airforce, Walt Disney Imagineering, PGA, Cowgirl Hall of Fame, Pan American World Airways, several Dot Com companies but was not directly responsible for the demise of any.

www.timberlinestudios.com

About the Author

Skip Halmes is a Montana native with life-long ties to ranching.   He, his wife, Holly and three children, Jake, Matt and Katie enjoy horses, cattle and the great outdoors on their ranch near Cascade. He is a part-time Outfitter and a full-time Financial Consultant with D.A. Davidson & Co. in Great Falls. To get a signed copy of *the Cow Whisperer,* e-mail:

lepleycreek@lepleycreekranch.com.

Proverbs 3:13 —— *Happy is the man who finds wisdom, and the man who gets understanding.* (on page 10 - the brands on the planks)

Proverbs 17:1 —— *Better is a dry crust of bread with quiet, than a house full of feasting with strife.* (on page 16 - look at the watermark under the cow and calf)

Proverbs 10:1 —— *A wise son makes his father glad, but a foolish son is a grief to his mother.* (on page 21 - look left of the saddle)

Proverbs 21:9 —— *It is better to live in the corner of a housetop, than in a house shared with a contentious woman.* (on page 26 - the watermark)

Proverbs 14:7 —— *If you're looking for advice, stay away from fools.* (on page 32 - under the boots)

Proverbs 24:10 —— *If you are weak in the day of adversity, you are weak indeed.* (on page 41 - watermark above the boots)

Proverbs 12:10 —— *A righteous man has regard for the life of his beast, but the mercy of the wicked is small.* (on page 47 - the watermark under the horse and his brands)

Proverbs 21:31 —— *The horse is made ready for the day of battle, but victory belongs to the lord.* (on page 56 - the brands on the cow)

Proverbs 20:1 —— *Wine is a mocker, strong drink a brawler; who ever is led astray by it is not wise.* (on page 60 - on the dutch oven and shadow)

Proverbs 18:9 —— *He who is slack in his work, is a brother to him who destroys.* (on page 68 - the watermark under the spurs)

Proverbs 19:5 —— *A false witness will not go unpunished, and he who utters lies will not escape.* (on page 74 - the watermark under the boots)

Genesis 1:26 —— *Then God said, "Let us make man in our image, after our likeness; and let him have dominion over the fish of the sea, and over the birds of the air, and over the cattle and over all the earth, and over every creeping thing that creeps upon the earth."* (page 81 - under the calf)

Proverbs 13:20 —— *He who walks with wise men becomes wise, but the companion of fools will suffer.* (on page 87 - the watermark beside the boots)

Proverbs 12:27 —— *A lazy man won't even dress the game he gets while hunting, but the diligent man makes good use of everything he gets.* (on page 92 - under the coyote)

Proverbs 31:10 —— *A good wife who can find? She is more precious than jewels.* (on page 96 - under the boots)

Proverbs 16:18 —— *Pride goes before destruction, and a haughty spirit before a fall.* (on page 98 & 102 - beside the boots and the brands on the planks)

Proverbs 17:12 —— *Let a man meet a she-bear robbed of her cubs, rather than a fool in his folly.* (on page 108 -the watermark under the buck horns)

Proverbs 21:20 —— *Precious treasure remains in a wise man's dwelling, but a foolish man devours it.* (on page 113 - the dutch oven and the shadow)

Proverbs 21:9 —— *A prudent man sees danger and hides himself; but the simple go on, and suffer for it.* (on page 118 - on the stirrup leather)

Proverbs 3:5 —— *Trust in the lord with all your heart, and do not rely on your own insight.* (page 124 - under the skull)

Proverbs 25:22 —— *For you will heap coals of fire on his head, and the lord will reward you.* (on page 130 - the watermark under the buck horns)

Proverbs 15:1 —— *A soft answer turns away wrath, but a harsh word stirs up anger.* (on page 134 - brands on the planks)

FOL

DEC 1 1 2024

158